Congratul...
Ma...

March 25, 2000

Learning to Live With the Love of Your Life

...And Loving It!

—♡—

May God bless your new family,
Mike + Jeanie Harshbarger
Michael + Sean

FOCUS ON THE FAMILY®

Neil Clark Warren, Ph.D.

Learning to Live With the Love of Your Life

...And Loving It!

Tyndale House Publishers, Wheaton, Illinois

LEARNING TO LIVE WITH THE LOVE OF YOUR LIFE...AND LOVING IT!
Copyright © 1995 by Neil Clark Warren. All rights reserved.

Library of Congress Cataloging-in-Publication Data

Warren, Neil Clark.
        Learning to Live with the Love of Your Life...and Loving It!/ Neil Clark Warren.
        p. cm.
    ISBN 1-56179-651-4
    1. Marriage.   2. Love.   I. Title.
    HQ734.W3177   1995
    646.7'008'655—dc20
        95-13726

CIP

A Focus on the Family book
Published by Tydale House Publishers, Wheaton, Illinois.

Unless otherwise stated, all Scripture quotes are taken from The Living Bible © 1971. Used by permission of Tyndale House Publishers, Inc., Wheaton, IL 60189. All rights reserved.

Editor: Keith Wall
Cover Design: Multnomah Graphics
Cover Illustration: Steve Diggs and Friends

Printed in the United States of America

This book was previously published under the title The Triumphant Marriage.

98 99 00 01 02/10 9 8 7 6 5 4 3 2 1

*This Book is Dedicated to
the 100 Couples
Who Have Worked So Hard
to Build TRIUMPHANT MARRIAGES
and Who Were So Generous
in the Sharing of Their Many Secrets*

Contents

Acknowledgments

When it comes to MARRIAGE, I am a man with a lot of acknowledgments to make. And when it comes to this book about highly successful marriages, I am aware of how much I owe to so many.

Our middle daughter, Dr. Luann Warren-Sohlberg, herself a psychologist with a strong interest in the study of marriage, did much of the literature review for this book—and talked with me about the theories and ideas at great length. Kevin Van Lant also combed the literature—and scored all the inventories.

Dee Otte was my administrative assistant during the data collection phase, and without her help and advice, I would never have enjoyed this project half as much.

Al Janssen, director of Book Publishing for Focus on the Family, has been an active guide and supporter throughout the process. Rolf Zettersten gave critical early help.

My editor and friend Keith Wall was a major contributor to this effort. I hope never to write another book without his highly competent and deeply meaningful help.

How can I say enough about the people who helped me find the 100 extremely successful couples all over the country? And there simply aren't enough words to convey my appreciation to the couples themselves. The fact is that this book has 201 authors.

My clients over these 30 years have played such a significant role in this project. Their stories are scrambled and coalesced, so they will not recognize themselves, but you can hear their voices in every chapter.

My wife, Marylyn, who has been the love of my life for 39 years, is my clearest-thinking critic and my strongest supporter. She and I have given our best effort to test every one of the secrets in this book.

For all kinds of reasons relating to my dream of a new day for marriage in North America, I want to thank my very close friend Tim Headington and my son-in-law Greg Forgatch.

Love Secrets for a
Triumphant Marriage

There are 107 million married persons in the United States, and most of them are aching for a better marriage. They desperately want their primary love relationship to be deeper and stronger, more fulfilling and more dependable. They want to feel better bonded with their mate, more consistently "in sync," and they want to know in their bones that their marriage is on its way to being healthier and more exciting—maybe even to being great.

This book is designed to help people make their marriages magnificent. The goal is to take ordinary marriages, or even miserable ones, and make them consistently better.

I take a revolutionary stance in relation to marriage. That stance is simply this: Marriage doesn't need to be chronically frustrating, constantly hurtful, and periodically—or routinely—ordinary. Marriage is the greatest institution ever invented! It can be good, or it can be great, but it should never be ordinary. I want to help you take your marriage from wherever it is and move it closer and closer to the highest level of satisfaction—to a level I refer to as *triumphant*. If your marriage is triumphant, it will overcome every last obstacle that stands in the way of its total success.

Two Hundred People in Extremely Successful Marriages Helped Me Write This Book

Helping people build great marriages is a huge undertaking, so I asked for assistance from the real pros—husbands and wives from across North America who are wonderfully happy in their marriages. I wrote to friends and colleagues all over the country and asked them to nominate the healthiest marriage they know. I ended up with spouses in 100 extremely healthy marriages, and I asked them everything I could think of about how they have become so successful.

Mind you, these are 100 triumphant marriages, and these men and women have spent years building their extraordinarily satisfying relationships. I sent each of these 200 spouses a long series of questions, and I found that the vast majority of them are sublimely happy. As a group of married people, they are deeply in love! Listen to some of them:

A woman from Illinois: *"I am 45 years old, and I met my husband 30 years ago. I fell in love with him then, and I am just as crazy about him today. He is the love of my life. He gives me confidence and strength and purpose. I'm lucky, we're lucky, and our kids are lucky."*

A man from California who has been married for 40 years: *"Joan is not just my wife, my lover, the mother of our child, and my life companion. She is also my best friend. We have continued to grow closer with each passing year, and our marriage is stronger now than it has ever been."*

A physician from Georgia: *"We have as close to a perfect marriage as anyone could have. Not because we are great communicators, or because sex is so great, or because of anything I have done. It's just one of those strange and rare miracles that happens—by the grace of God."*

A 36-year-old woman in California: *"I know with all my heart that I married the very best person for me. In fact, I think he is the most supportive and caring man I know. He has helped me tear down the walls that surround me, and even though I sometimes feel that some still remain, he loves me in spite of them."*

A woman from Minnesota: *"There are certain 'bedrock' qualities and strengths that I saw in Lee, even during our courtship, that are still a part of him today. These qualities are deeper and stronger now, more distilled by the action of life's experiences and growing faith. I've seen him in all kinds of situations with many different types of people, and my love and respect for him continue to grow. I'm so blessed and so proud to be his wife."*

How Hard Is Marriage?

For most people, it is incredibly difficult to build a great marriage. It requires a high degree of focus, careful instruction, and a giant supply of motivation. Far too many couples give up when they encounter serious challenges. In fact, the "give-up" rate is so high that marriage failure has reached epidemic proportions. One prominent marriage expert predicts that of all the marriages that take place in the United States this year, 66 percent will end in separation or divorce.

There is no doubt, however, that hard work pays off. Our 100 couples regularly talked about the "cost-benefit ratio" of their marriage:

A man from New York state: *"I can't imagine being married to anyone else, but this came after years of hard and committed work. It was all worth it. The job of a successful marriage is uncommonly difficult, but the prize is equally wonderful."*

A 31-year-old woman: *"I truly love being married, and I truly love my husband with all my heart. I know that God chose him for me because no other man has ever made me feel so loved, so wanted, and so good about myself. Marriage is not easy, but all the work you put into it—and all the prayer—is truly worth it when you are blessed with a great relationship, great friends, beautiful children, and a love that will last a lifetime."*

The Central Role of Love

Every marriage expert knows that hard work and determination aren't the only ingredients that lead to a great marriage. Some couples work incredibly hard on their marriages, but they are left hungering for something significantly better.

Our 100 couples made it clear what they think is the central issue. My questionnaire contained 13 factors that are vital for a marriage to be highly successful, and the vast majority of the couples ranked "being in love" as the most important quality of all.

A 1990 Roper Institute survey supports this conclusion. In that poll, 3,000 women and 1,000 men were selected randomly from across America. From the same set of 13 crucial qualities that make for a good marriage, the most popular answer of all (87 percent of the women and 84 percent of the men) was "being in love."

The critical question about every marriage is a question about *love!* Whether a marriage becomes great or not depends entirely on whether two people learn to love each other well—whether they learn love's secrets and develop the necessary skills to implement them. This kind of love can energize a marriage and fill it with vitality and health. It can create a relational fabric that will make the marital life supremely worth living—even when problems arise.

What Is Love Anyway?

My own empirical research and clinical experience are strongly in support of a triangular theory of love developed by Robert J. Sternberg of Yale University. Professor Sternberg has argued:

> Love has three components: (a) intimacy, which encompasses the feelings of closeness, connectedness, and bondedness one experiences in loving relationships; (b) passion, which encompasses the drives that lead to romance, physical attraction, and sexual consummation; and (c) decision/commitment, which encompasses in the short term, the decision that one loves another, and in the long term, the commitment to maintain that love.[1]

If these three components constitute most or all of what it means to love someone, then we have taken a giant step forward in understanding the "mystery" of marriage. If the fundamental purpose of marriage is to provide a context in which a deeper, purer, richer form of love can be enjoyed—and if love is all about intimacy, passion, and commitment—we are ready to focus our skill-building efforts on these specific dimensions. The payoff for those who succeed in developing these skills is a level of human experience beyond our fondest dreams.

In fact, it is the possibility of attaining this satisfying payoff that explains why people keep getting married. Even though so many marriages hit the rocks and break apart, the potential of marriage is eagerly pursued by virtually everyone. More than 94 percent of all Americans marry at least once, and 75 percent of divorced persons remarry—half of them within two years.[2] You would have to say that marriage has been a terrible disappointment for a high percentage of Americans, but its attractiveness remains surprisingly strong.

Part of the reason for this revolves around how we're built. There is a profound sense in most of us that we can know a deeper level of love and a greater sense of completeness when we find that person of the opposite sex with whom we can enjoy a life-changing experience of intimacy, passion, and commitment. When a man finds his woman and a woman finds her man, all they need for a magnificent union is the insight and skill involved in developing these three components.

If these secrets are never mastered, marriage will be devastatingly disappointing and empty. But any union in which the "secrets of love" provide the yarn out of which the marriage fabric is woven promises a significantly better payoff for time and energy investments than any other human enterprise.

Ten Proven "Love Secrets" for Building a Great Marriage

After 30 years of clinical work, I am convinced I know the secrets of long-lasting and deeply satisfying love. I've taken my clinical discoveries, my reading of thousands of research studies and theoretical articles, my study of Jewish and Christian teachings, my experiences in a marriage of 36 years, my close-up observations of the marriages of our three daughters and a score of intimate friends—along with the enormous wisdom of these 100 couples I keep mentioning—and I've distilled all of this into a set of 10 straightforward "secrets." If followed carefully, these secrets can revolutionize your love relationship and make your marriage more and more fulfilling.

Moreover, I believe that a brilliant marriage can be built by any two people who are willing to learn and practice this set of skills. The key word is *learn!* The notion that a marriage "just works" or "just doesn't work" is antiquated. A great marriage requires carefully informed and precisely drilled participants who envision what they can have with one another and then set about the task of producing it in the relationship.

Is All This Grounded in Reality?

I don't have a naive bone in my body when it comes to marriage—not after 30 years of watching every kind of marriage catastrophe. I have listened to hundreds of couples go after each other with words and ideas that were more like grenades and mortar shells than thoughtful expressions designed to save marriages. I have struggled and fought, cried and prayed over marriages at every level of decay. No one should assume that I've never seen a marriage as complex, as frustrating, as hopeless, and as strange as theirs.

One of the strongest conclusions I've reached after all of this experience is that the epidemic of marital breakdown in North America today is not the fault of the marriage institution! Marriage has taken a bum rap because a lot of untrained, undisciplined, uninspired, and sometimes unhealthy people have tried it and failed. As well-meaning as many of these people are, they are mostly without a clue about how to improve their marriages. They just keep trying the same old strategies. They keep hoping that somehow their marriage will finally work, that their spouse will change, that something magical will save their painful, miserable relationship.

It would be as silly for a beginning golfer to expect to become a professional by just playing a few rounds as it is to expect to have a satisfying marriage by finding a willing partner and getting married. You need solid training to be good at making a marriage work! You need to know exactly what a triumphant marriage requires. And you need to practice until you're *very* good at it.

Your Marriage Can Become 10 Percent Better
Every Year You Live

A highly respected friend of mine is the CEO of a successful company. He took up tennis a few years ago, and he became incredibly good at it. I asked him how he became so proficient. He told me he searched for the best tennis instructor in Los Angeles. Having secured this teacher's services, he took two-hour lessons four times a week for two years.

I then asked about his progress. Without saying a word, he held his hand out in front of him with his palm down and his fingers close together. He started two feet above the ground and kept moving his hand upward until it was well above his head. His summary words to me were: "Good teacher, hard work, dramatic results."

If you're motivated to work on your marriage like my friend was motivated to work on his tennis game, your marriage can grow as dramatically as his tennis skills did. Once you know the crucial secrets, it will all depend on the amount of motivation you have. If you're sick and tired of being miserable in your marriage, grab your partner, and let's spend a few hours together working to build a great marriage for the two of you. If the idea of a triumphant marriage catches your fancy, then the plan outlined in this book is precisely what you need. In fact, if you will work at this plan, I promise your marriage can become 10 percent better this next year, and every year thereafter. And it could be much greater than that.

This country could certainly use a few hundred thousand solid, healthy, fulfilling marriages; maybe yours could be one of them. It's time for us to be done with average, mediocre, painful marriages! Let's set our sights on brilliant marriages! I'm convinced the 10 secrets in this book are everything you need to know, and I'll take you carefully and thoroughly through each of them. Then we'll go after the prize with every ounce of determination and courage we have. If you're willing to work, really work, we won't stop until your marriage is well on its way to greatness!

Dream a Dream

Construct a Vision of Everything You Believe Your Marriage Can Be

"I dreamed some dreams: to remain passionate, to work our way to a comfortable station in life, to have children (who would, of course, be perfect!), to travel together, and we often talked of 'growing old together' so we'd always be with someone who remembered us in younger years."

—a 43-year-old woman from New Jersey

"I envisioned a husband I was crazy about, a home I cherished, kids I adored, an interesting career and service to mankind. I wanted someone to share that vision with me. Because our visions meshed so closely, I think we have been very fortunate. Twenty-one years later, my priorities haven't changed much."

—a woman from Washington State

A few years ago, when the Los Angeles Rams football team lost to the Chicago Bears in the National Football League playoffs, Coach John Robinson took all the blame.

"The reason we lost," he said, "is because I was never able to communicate to the team a vision of our winning. And without a vision of being able to do something, you can't do anything."

Just like football teams, when spouses do not have a vision, they risk losing—and losing at something far more important than a game.

On the other hand, what an enormous qualitative difference it makes for two lovers to dream together about their marriage! Too often, people "wander into" this high-requirement game of marriage with a totally inadequate dream. Without this kind of guiding vision, they become easy targets for disappointment, temptation, conflict, boredom, and confusion.

I still remember like it was yesterday the time Josh and Lindsay called me for premarital counseling. They were both in their early 30s, never married before, and they came from difficult family situations. Even though they felt sure their love was strong and healthy, they didn't want to fail like their parents had. They wanted to check out their relationship with someone like me.

During our first session, while I was still learning all about how they met and fell in love, I asked them a question I often ask of couples who are married or even thinking about it.

"Tell me what your life together will be like 10 years from now," I said.

They looked at each other and smiled—like this was a question they had talked about before and thoroughly enjoyed discussing.

"One of the things I like so much about Josh and me," Lindsay began, "is the way we think together about our future. We think about how life can be deep-down satisfying for Josh, and we think about how life can be thoroughly fulfilling for me. And we talk about our relationship—how we can build it and make it healthy and strong for both of us."

"It sounds like this is unique for you, like it hasn't happened with anyone else you've dated," I responded.

"Oh, it hasn't!" she said. "I've been in several relationships, but never one in which we looked out into the future for more than six months or so. Josh and I dream some big dreams, and we have a vision of the kind of life we want to have together."

"Okay," I said, "tell me some of the specifics. What do you want to have happen?"

"Well, let's start with Lindsay," Josh broke in. "She wants to be a mom, but she also wants to finish her doctoral studies in Russian literature. She's active in her church, and she wants to stay very involved with some of their outreach programs."

"And Josh, don't forget the traveling we want to do," she said.

Josh smiled at her and said, "That's *our* dream for the *two* of us. Right now I'm just talking about you. It may take us the rest of this session to spell out all of our dreams for *you!*"

They both laughed, and so did I, because what I knew already was that they had a great vision together. Show me a couple with a big dream for their individual and corporate lives, one that involves a deep sensitivity to both partners' needs, and I'll show you a couple on their way to a triumphant marriage.

The Theory Behind Marital Dreams and Visions

Dreams and visions stimulate the brain and mobilize the action centers. Whatever it is that you dream about with regularity, you will begin to hope for. Hope stimulates planning. Planning produces behavior designed to move you forward. This brings progress. It all begins with a dream!

When two people dream and envision together, they merge the resources of their deepest, most positive centers. They each have tremendous personal power when they access the core emotions and longings in their individual centers. When they pool this power and focus it for the benefit of all three of them—each of them individually and the two of them as a couple—they become significantly stronger than they could be as two separate individuals.

It is this corporate strength that contributes to the greatness and the excitement of marriage. When this strength is mobilized, the partners are able to overcome momentary adversity, withstand temporary stalemates, push temptations aside, and prove victorious over every kind of difficulty. Apart from the inspirational power of these merged centers, marriage automatically becomes a defensive game designed to hold off defeat. With this kind of defensiveness, the best a marriage can do is "hold its own." Progress and movement are in short supply because the dream either doesn't exist or has become terribly unfocused.

The Link Between Dreaming and Romance

Dreaming and envisioning are the essence of romance! Show me a couple who dreams about their future together—or tells someone else about their dreams—and I will show you a couple who is deeply in love. People who help each other access and focus their individual and corporate dreams are vital to one another. There is nothing in the world so attractive as someone who will dream with us, merge their dreams with our own, clarify the path toward the actualization of the dream, and lock their arms into ours while walking the path.

The best marriages I know involve two people who have a well-formed vision of the life they are pursuing together. I've noticed that these people thoroughly enjoy dreaming together—and planning a way to make their dreams come true.

At the center of all this dreaming and planning is a constantly recurring theme: "I want the future to be good for you. If it is not good for you, it cannot be good for us. Whatever is healthy and good for you, we will find a way to make it work in our life together." Do you hear that theme? "I want it to be good for *you!*" Being cared for this way, if it is unselfish and mutual, is at the core of romance.

Three Essential Criteria for Healthy Marital Dreaming

When I ask a couple about the dreams they have for their life together, I listen very closely as they spread that vision out in front of me. After all these years of hearing hundreds of people share their "marital destinations," I have become especially alert to three aspects of these dreams. As I listen, I ask myself three questions about the vision the couple has:

1. **Is the dream equally inclusive of each of them and their life together?** I feel a sense of shame when I think about the beginning vision my wife, Marylyn, and I had for our life together. Granted, it was a number of years ago, but there is no excuse for how heavily we emphasized my career and my life, often at the expense of our life together. Somehow, the dream for her life was supposed to be a part of my life. We simply focused too little on those parts that would provide deep satisfaction for her own personal needs. Fortunately, we have corrected this glaring error in our marriage. I now know that if this oversight remains unchanged in a marriage, one or both partners will suffer terribly.

2. **Is the dream broad enough?** By this I mean does it cover enough of the totality of life? I look for a strong emphasis on more than just those common dreams that are a result of social conditioning. There is nothing wrong with having kids, buying a nice house, achieving career success,

and traveling to far-off places. But there may be something narrow and superficial about the experience of reaching these goals.

I want to know if people have given thought to the development of their spiritual sides as they contemplate their future. I am interested in whether their journey-together dream gives plenty of weight to their skill for sharing more and more generously with each other from the deepest parts of their inner lives. And I look for the place of service to less fortunate people and to their communities. To produce a brilliant marriage, the dream must be broad enough to include others and deep enough to reach the spiritual realm.

3. **Is there evidence that both partners are strongly committed to the dream they have for their life together?** Sometimes, one person is so obviously the leader that you wonder if the other person is "on board." When you begin to sense that there is a deeply shared commitment to the dream, you start believing in the dream's power to do great things for the marriage.

Every Couple Needs to Have a Dream for Their Life Together

I hold that *every* couple needs to take conscious responsibility for choosing the course their marriage will follow. Goodness knows that their marriage will follow some course—even if it's around in circles. And the best course is likely to be the one they choose together at every point along the way.

Sally and Jim had been married for 33 years when they came to me for a marital checkup. They told me that nothing was dramatically wrong with their life together, but they just wanted to be sure they were maximizing their marital power. I simply fell in love with this couple, because their dedication to excellence was so strong and their awareness of the great possibilities for their marriage was so well established.

As they told me about their lives, they kept using the word *blessed*.

"We have three wonderful children," Sally said, "and we feel so blessed by them."

They enumerated one "feeling of blessedness" after another. If I could repeat them all, you might wonder why they came to see a psychologist in the first place.

It was Jim who began to develop the issue that occupied us for a few sessions. "Our youngest child, Carol, finished college last year," he said, "and she's now working in Washington, D.C. Frankly, Sally and I have experienced a surprising emptiness with all the kids gone. And now I hope to retire in four or five years, and Sally is having some trouble getting used to this whole new phase in our lives."

As I talked to this healthy couple, what we all recognized was that it had been a long time since they had envisioned their lives together five, 10, or 15 years ahead. Their lack of a *current*, carefully developed plan for them as individuals, and especially for their marriage—a plan they both believed in deeply—left them feeling the anxiety that comes from being unfocused.

Obviously, even the best of marital visions grows stale and out of date. A reworking of the vision is a continual necessity. Sometimes, complete remodeling rather than merely redecoration is required, and nervousness sets in for one or both partners. Everyone needs to end up sensing that their individual concerns have been listened to fully.

The point of all this is that *every* couple needs to have a vision for their future, and they need to keep that vision up to date and carefully focused.

What About Living One Day at a Time?

Some of the partners in the 100 highly successful marriages I studied said that they "simply try to live their lives one day at a time." One man even said that he steers away from planning for the future, preferring to deal with the issues of life as they present themselves today.

After I sat for a long time and studied the matter of "vision for the future" versus "living one day at a time," I came to three conclusions.

First, some people have a very well-worked-out vision for how they conduct their lives—but they like to think that their strategy is actually moment-by-moment. As I studied the lives of these people, I became convinced that "one day at a time" is a slogan that governs their thinking, but the health of their marriages indicates that all kinds of other "agreements" about the future have been worked out with their spouses. For instance, they get up every morning and do all kinds of things for each other. She gets coffee for both of them, and he gets the newspaper. She takes some meat out of the freezer for dinner, and he calls the travel agent about their trip next month. They are living their life one day at a time, but their coordination in the midst of complexity is often the result of a quiet, unassuming vision of their life together—a vision that guides them into the future, even if that future is only the next few hours.

Second, some married people live with a lot of fear about the future, and they would just as soon avoid thinking about tomorrow. When two people are deeply and vitally in love, they become wildly important to one another.

They don't even want to think about the profound awfulness of something happening to one of them and their being separated. If they take life "just one day at a time," their awareness of the risk that the future holds seems more manageable.

Finally, it occurs to me that there is after all a kind of wisdom about living life—and being in a marriage—one day at a time, but *only* if the fundamental issues have been largely decided. In the New Testament, Jesus carefully instructs His hearers: "So don't be anxious about tomorrow. God will take care of your tomorrow too. Live one day at a time" (Matthew 6:34). But His teaching comes in the middle of an incredible sermon with strong emphases on God being in charge of the world, people being deeply authentic and strong, and loving values guiding all our interactions with one another. When one's vision about the future is this well established, living one day at a time seems entirely reasonable and wise.

Having a vision for the future does not preclude living one day at a time. In fact, working toward the fulfillment of dreams and having a clear destination may help you make the most of each day. Without direction, one day blends into the next as you live only for the here and now. But working toward a grand goal can give every day meaning and significance, because you're moving, step by step, toward the realization of your vision.

The Relationship Between Dreams and Reality

My years of clinical work have convinced me that all of us have access to an incredible computer . . . and it's located right between our ears. I have watched people put this computer to a test, and the results have been startling. Yet I suspect that most of us utilize far too little of our brain's capacity when it comes to envisioning our own future, the future of the person we love more than all others, and our corporate future with this person. We seldom test the limits of our amazing instrument. We don't even come close to challenging it.

Moreover, I have found that the brain can not only conceive big dreams but also help us plan to achieve them. Develop a big plan for your life together, and then get about the thoroughly enjoyable task of setting your brain free to plan and achieve the well-designed marital estate you have envisioned.

Still, without limiting the scope of our dreams, we do need to remain balanced in our approach. Dreams do need to have some realism about them. For instance, there are all kinds of things I would like to do that are too far beyond reality for me ever to dream about. My dad loved baseball, and he taught me to love baseball, too. I have often thought about how satisfying it would be to own a major league baseball team, but the price of a team is totally beyond anything that would ever be possible for me. In fact, the price of a season ticket is even a big stretch!

But realism must not totally control our dreaming. If it does, our dreams will have no ability to lift us off the ground and help us fly. Dreams and visions help us most when they are allowed to formulate in our heads without immediate attention to workable operational plans. The fact is that for most of us, the Gestapo-like authority of reality never goes away for long. There will inevitably come a time when we will hang on to a dream or let it go, and the letting-go decision will be governed by the demands of reality that come from the most cautious part of our brains.

My own experience is that individuals and couples in our society dream far too little. From an early age, most of us are subtly or not-so-subtly encouraged to be realistic. We become so submissive to reality that we shut down the dreamer in us. We shut off some of the most exciting possibilities that might have occurred for us.

Maybe that is why the Calvin and Hobbes comic strip is so intensely popular. Bill Watterson has developed in Calvin a little boy who dreams wildly and consistently. Hobbes—a small, stuffed tiger who comes alive only for Calvin—is part of the boy's dreaming. Hobbes constantly finds himself in the middle of Calvin's whimsical imaginings. The popularity of this comic strip for so many of us points to the liberating, exhilarating effects of letting the brake off our dreaming process. Most of us admire the ability to let our imaginations run free and conjure up fanciful dreams.

Of course, I'm not suggesting that we dream unrealistically about our marriages and then chase those dreams unsuccessfully for much of our lives. There is a pathological quality to that process. But sometimes we play life in our marriages far too cautiously! In the name of protecting ourselves from failing, we seldom succeed. We bore ourselves to death. Sometimes, marriages do literally die of boredom. I've watched it happen. Two people stop dreaming together. They lose any interest in choosing their destination. They become far too accepting of "whatever comes," and whatever comes often isn't much.

One of the critical requirements of healthy marital dreams is that they stretch our corporate ability to plan. Our dream together needs to be big enough so that we are forced to find a way to actualize it.

Sometimes I wonder if it is really possible to dream such a big dream that it is actually beyond what we can finally attain. In fact, I have begun to sense that the greatness of a marriage is correlated with the size and passion of the dream two lovers have for their lives together. Magnificent marriages involve two people who dream magnificently. The partners encourage each other to dig deeper and dream bigger, and in the process they get in touch with a level of being and doing that otherwise would be far beyond them.

Dreams and Values

Dreams are partially masked strategies designed to meet basic needs. Values are considerations that help us determine the long-term effect of pursuing a given strategy for the satisfaction of one of our needs.

For instance, let's say that you have a need to be important so that you can feel good about yourself. You dream of becoming outlandishly wealthy so that you can buy and sell with abandon. You're just sure that if this dream came true for you, you would feel really good about who you are.

But one value that has been proven over and over concerns the superficial internal effects of accumulating material things. Specifically, the need to feel important usually doesn't get met when the dream of becoming wealthy comes true.

So what do you do when you are in a marriage, and your partner keeps dreaming dreams for him- or herself—and for the two of you—that strike you as violating your values? I believe that the harmonizing of dreams and values is an essential part of the process of capturing a marital vision. Sometimes it is right where dreams and values meet that negotiation becomes most intense. And that's fine!

Choosing which dreams you want to dream together is a big part of the joy and excitement that comes from the enterprise. The relationship takes on real substance in the process of both people discovering their basic needs, developing the dreams that are designed to provide the satisfaction for those needs, and then checking out the congruence of those dreams with their individual value systems.

So How Do We Learn to Dream Together?

If you are in a marriage that suffers from a lack of vision about the future, you may be eager to remedy your deficit. But you wonder how to proceed. You are not at all alone.

Peter and Linda came to me with a story I hear often. Linda had become progressively more frustrated with their marriage over the past few years.

Her frustration had nothing to do with a lack of money, or with heated arguments about how to raise their three kids, or any of the more obvious problems marriages often experience.

"Peter and I have just drifted apart over the years," Linda said. "He works 12 to 15 hours a day, seldom gets home before 8:00 or 8:30 at night, is totally exhausted, seems obsessive about his law practice, and often appears to have little interest in me or my life. It's like we have a financial partnership, a parenting partnership, a periodic sexual partnership—but we have almost totally lost touch with each other."

Peter sat quietly through all of this, and then he sat up straight. "How can you say that, Linda?" he said with an edge to his voice. "We went out to the club for dinner last weekend, and I'm often home on Saturday afternoons and Sunday mornings!"

Despite Peter's protests, I could tell after only one session that Linda was right. They had indeed drifted away from each other. They were more like strangers than lovers. All the externals were in place, but the romance was missing. The love that once made them giddy with one another had dwindled to a shadow of its former self.

I asked them the time-tested question: "Where do the two of you hope to be 10 years from now?"

They looked at each other and then at me. There was at least 60 seconds of silence. Peter took off his coat. Linda moved around on the sofa and smoothed her skirt.

It was as if this question caught them totally by surprise. They had been spending all their energy on survival—making it through *today* and *this week*. It had been several years since they had even raised the question about their destination together.

During these years, of course, all the romance had drained out of their relationship. They each had their individual responsibilities, and they were managing those as well as they knew how. But there was virtually no time for their marriage. Peter was totally absorbed by a law practice that was about to devour him. Meanwhile, Linda, the love of his life, the one with whom he actually wanted to build a brilliant marriage, had become for him a nagger. He tried to keep her happy by meeting at least the minimum of her needs, but now he was failing even that.

Not that Linda was blameless. Her days were stuffed full of duties, responsibilities and obligations. Two mornings of tennis with her friends helped relieve the stress, but sometimes even these fun activities contributed to her feeling of being smothered by her schedule. Even though she complained bitterly about Peter and his lack of interest in her, the fact was that she didn't have much time for him either.

Their marriage, they both knew, had become mediocre. Their relationship with each other had, through the years, been squeezed into a small room, then into a closet, and now it was on a shelf in the basement.

I imagine many of these thoughts were rattling around in their heads as they contemplated my question about their dream for their future.

Finally, Peter looked up at me. "Could you state the question again?" he asked sheepishly. He had returned from a fast jog around his "inner neighborhood."

Slowly, I repeated the question: "Where do the two of you hope to be 10 years from now?" For the rest of that hour, and for four additional hours, we began to compose their best response to that question. Here is the way I tried to help Peter and Linda formulate their vision:

1. I encouraged them to picture themselves in the future and to get a sense of what would likely be true for them in 10 years. Peter would be 48, and Linda 47. Their son, Matt, would be in his second year of college, and their daughter, Jamie, would be finishing high school. Their youngest son, Pete Jr., would just be heading into high school. Peter would have been a partner in his law firm for 12 years, perhaps a senior partner by then. All their parents would be over 70, and Linda's parents would be in their early 80s. Linda would be much freer in relation to kids but more responsible for her aging parents. They began to get a picture of what "10 years from now" would be like.

2. Then I had them spend some time *together* thinking about where *each* would like to be in 10 years and where they would like their marriage to be. Both Peter and Linda decided that they would like for Peter to pull way back from his law practice. His goal, he decided, was to write a book and spend some quality time learning to play the clarinet. Also, he would really enjoy working part time in a local law program designed to protect the rights of disadvantaged people.

Linda was hungry to get back to school herself. She would start slowly and then pick up speed as the kids got older. Her dream: graduate training in horticulture. She wanted to become an expert on the plant life she already loved. And when it came to their marriage, every additional session brought a new flood of dreams for the resurrection of their love, the renewing of their closeness. Peter even put together a five-area marital enrichment plan on his computer, which, when Linda looked at it spread out on the coffee table in my office, brought a lot of tears. It was like the romance was return-ing to their life, and she was trembling and celebrating with delight.

3. Next I asked them to prepare a chart showing the 10-year period, broken down into six-month segments. On this chart, they were to enter their vision as they hoped it would unfold over time. Ten years became such a short period when they began to introduce all the goals they had for themselves and their marriage.

4. I then asked them to list the obstacles they expected to encounter in the implementation of their plan. There were many, the primary one being the momentum of their out-of-control lives. I pushed them to write out *every* impediment they imagined.

5. The next step was to devise a way to deal with each of the challenges they had listed. This section was built around the matter of *discipline*. We talked at length about the kind of discipline two people need to actualize their vision. They committed themselves to some life-changing discipline!

6. I asked Peter and Linda to each write a page about how they would feel—10 years from now—if this plan were realized. Their statements were full of excitement and celebration, and their love for each other took on a whole new look. The very act of formulating a vision together had renewed their hope. Their estimate of the quality of their marriage, if they lived out their vision, was full of rich and life-affirming adjectives.

It is frighteningly easy in a demanding world for two people who are married to become distant and lost. The story of Peter and Linda may reflect your own experience. The act of reconsidering your destination may cause you to re-evaluate how very crucial is your life with each other. You may begin to sense that you are simply not willing to settle for what your marriage is currently becoming. Formulating a vision for your future together is an exercise that every couple needs to engage in—and preferably every year.

When Your Partner Won't Cooperate

Obviously, a vision for the future of your marriage will be significantly stronger if both spouses are involved in formulating and actualizing it. But I've had scores of married individuals come to me for marriage counseling even though their partner refused to participate.

Sometimes an uncooperative spouse can doom a marriage. But not always! In fact, I've watched scores of marriages take on new strength on the basis of just one person's active dreaming and praying for their marriage. When that one person becomes crystal clear about a great and worthy vision for their own life and for the marriage, and when that person sets his or her mind in the direction of the chosen destination, all kinds of good things can happen.

A 57-year-old woman named Marjorie called me one day for help with her "tired" marriage. She explained that her three children were on their own now and that her husband was unwilling to work on the marriage with her, but she desperately wanted things to be better. She came to me for several months, and I have seldom witnessed anyone more eager to work hard—even with zero cooperation from her spouse. I helped her develop a five-year plan for her marriage, one that she could work on all by herself.

Then one day a miracle happened. I answered the phone, and a shy man on the other end said, "This is Henry. My wife is Marjorie, and I believe she has been seeing you for counseling."

"Henry!" I said, almost unable to control my excitement. "How can I help you?"

"I wasn't willing to come with my wife for counseling at first," he said, "but I can't believe how much she has changed during the last few months. Maybe I had better get started, too."

I just wanted to hug him. But the person I really wanted to hug was Marjorie! What courage it takes to give everything you have in an effort to make your marriage better—even though your spouse hangs back and refuses to get involved.

Over the next few months, after Henry got started, Marjorie began to see her once-tired marriage come alive. It was another in a long string of stories about the incredible influence that one dedicated partner can have on his or her spouse.

So if you are the one longing to have a far better marriage, don't give up! Rather, do everything I have talked about in this chapter—to the best of your ability—and then work to make *your* vision a reality. You may be shocked at the dramatic results.

A Vision for Your Marriage

Wherever you are in your marriage currently, I am convinced that any investment you make in building a great dream for you and your partner will pay generous dividends. I encourage you to think long and hard about the kind of life that will provide for each of you individually—and for the two of you together—the level of satisfaction you seek. I have two friends who carry the following vision in their wallets at all times:

Greg and Jackie hereby commit themselves to the following: (1) to love each other under every circumstance for as long as they live; (2) to search after meaning and satisfaction together wherever it may be found; (3) to support and encourage each other at every turn of life; (4) to love their kids generously and personally, and to raise them wisely; (5) to be involved in serving others, especially the underprivileged; (6) to respond actively and enthusiastically to the love and guidance of God.

I asked Greg and Jackie if I could include their vision in this book. They agreed and wanted me to point out that an early version of this vision was worked out before they got married, while he was in the army, and that they believe it has had more to do with their extremely healthy marriage than any other single factor.

Let me stress this point: Show me a couple with a big dream for their individual and corporate lives, one that involves a deep sensitivity to both of their needs, and I'll show you a couple on their way to a triumphant marriage.

Get Tough

A Triumphant Marriage Requires Two Strong, Skillful, Thoroughly Committed Partners

"Commitment and determination are what I believe love is—not some sweet feeling. No matter what we have experienced so far, no matter how hard or painful, we have been committed to each other and have trusted that circumstances would not change that commitment."

—a woman from Washington State

"If we hadn't been committed to God, to the institution of marriage, and to each other, we might not have made it. Such commitment is a good foundation on which romantic love may grow. If you try to base the marriage on emotions, you are in trouble."

—a man from Alabama

Does one of the following describe marriage for you?

- You fell in love, the question was "popped," the wedding was a wonderful success, and marriage is now a continual joyride for both of you.

- You fell in love, the wedding was a mixture of stress and success, and marriage is a wagon-train trip across the plains and over the mountains to the old west.

- You fell in love, the wedding was a series of problems to be solved, and marriage is a marathon run on a hot, summer day through hill country.

- You fell in love, the wedding was an expensive headache, and marriage is a bloody gunfight at the O.K. Corral.

Which of these scenarios would characterize your marriage? Has it been a joyride or a gunfight—or something in between? The majority of married people I know, especially the ones who are still alive and married, talk about their experience as "somewhere in between," not exactly a joyride all the time, but not a gunfight either.

I'm fully aware that a few married people describe their relationships as "nothing but wonderful" or "a sleigh ride on a snowy night with the bells on the horses jingling and the sound of a carol-singing choir in the background." Some people believe that marriage can be a perpetual joyride. That may be true for some, but not for most people.

For most people, the demands of marriage are mind-boggling. It requires all the energy you can give it—and then it asks for more. It involves a continual need for negotiation and compromise, for give and more give.

Mind you, I'm a big believer in marriage. I have never seen happier, more deeply satisfied people than men and women who have made their marriages work. But neither have I met many people in highly successful marriages who got there without an enormous expenditure of energy and courage and determination. There were times when they simply had to be "willful." Virtually every successful marriage requires all kinds of willpower. Sometimes issues arise and the partners don't have the necessary skills to manage them. They essentially have two choices: give up and run away, or get about the task of developing the required skills. Partners with willpower always adopt the second alternative. They wouldn't think of giving up. They are ready to go to work on the problem, ready to do whatever they must to keep their marriage healthy for a lifetime.

The foundation of willpower is a set of marital promises. It is this set of promises that serves as the steel structure of every great marriage. Both partners need to know exactly what they originally promised to each other, and they need to be *currently* committed to those promises so that their willpower will always be stronger than *any* opposing force.

Marriage doesn't just happen! It takes a solid set of decisions, a huge amount of skill, and enormous willpower. I contend that people in extremely healthy marriages *built* those marriages just as you build a mammoth bridge or a skyscraper. They made their marriage triumphant because they simply wouldn't settle for less. It doesn't matter at all to them how much back-breaking work it requires; if it were necessary, they would do a thousand times more. Their willpower gives them this kind of toughness.

Commitment: The Cornerstone of a Triumphant Marriage

Marriage is so difficult and requires so much toughness that, as a society, we ask persons entering marriage to take some hard-hitting, heavy-duty vows. We know how easy it will be for them to give up along the way, to claim that they didn't know marriage could be so demanding. We gather into small or large groups just to hear them take these vows, and the people who are already married know that there are going to be times when these newlyweds will have to refer back to their vows—with the future of their marriage hanging in the balance.

Unfortunately, these vows are often treated with incredible superficiality. Maybe that's because society has only recently recognized the deadly serious dilemma we're in when it comes to marital instability. With a divorce rate that has us reeling, our nation is waking up fast to how fiercely difficult it is to make a marriage work. We are beginning to recognize how grossly we have underestimated the difficulty of marriage and how underequipped marital participants have been. As a nation, we have reached the edge of total family collapse.

When I read the inventories of the 200 persons in our "advisory group," I was overwhelmed at the frequency with which they emphasized the critical importance of commitment. One man said it succinctly: "Our lives are the sum total of our commitments. Commitment is the essence of what marriage is all about." More than 90 percent of the respondents echoed his words. Everywhere I turned in these inventories, I heard the same powerful opinion: "Marriage demands toughness, and toughness proceeds out of commitment. No marriage will ever be stronger than the commitment that serves as its infrastructure."

Jeanette and Robert Lauer published the results of their powerful study a few years ago.[1] They surveyed 351 couples who had been married 15 or more years. Of the 351 couples, 300 said they were happily married. Each husband and wife responded individually to a questionnaire that included 39 statements and questions about marriage. They were asked to select from their answers "the ones that best explained why their marriages had lasted." Out of 39 important reasons, two of the four rated "most important" for both men and women were: "Marriage is a long-term commitment" and "Marriage is sacred."

Robert Sternberg, the Yale professor I quoted in the first chapter, has frequently cited commitment as crucial to a successful marriage. Here are his words:

> Loving relationships almost inevitably have their ups and downs, and there may be times in such relationships when the decision/commitment component is all or almost all that keeps the relationship going. This component can be essential for getting through hard times and returning to better ones. In ignoring it or separating it from love, one may be missing exactly that component of loving relationships that enables one to get through the hard times as well as the easy ones.[2]

It is a tough-sounding vow that society asks people entering marriage to take, and it should be. If they are to be successful, they must be prepared for a major contest. They need to be trained and toughened—and why not? We require our citizens to prepare long and hard for careers. We put soldiers, policemen, and firemen through rigorous training programs. We expect athletes and athletic teams to practice for months so they will be equal to the challenge of competition. But we are in the habit of sending persons into marriage with virtually no understanding of the challenges they will face. The inevitable massacre is tragically predictable! The bottom line is that marriage is often tougher than marital participants are. That can change.

Skills Necessary for a Triumphant Marriage

We must understand that commitment alone is only part of the equation for a triumphant marriage. Commitment must lead to skill development. I have never studied a great marriage in which I viewed the partners as anything less than profoundly skillful. It's crucial to recognize, though, that much of the time these skills were learned and developed *after* the marriage began. Often, the development of the skills came in response to a crisis or a series of crises.

Many persons in our group of 100 healthy marriages encountered enormous problems in their marriages, and in response to those problems, they learned marriage-saving skills. If those skills were learned unusually well, the crisis was not only handled, but the marriage also took on a new level of strength and satisfaction that would not have been available if the crisis had not emerged. Marriage-saving skills became vital resources in building a great relationship.

What are those skills that people must learn if their marriage is to survive and move toward greatness? They are all the secrets I discuss in this book, such as creating a great vision with your lover, resolving conflicts before they dissolve the marriage, communicating with each other so that harmony rather than chaos characterizes the relationship, and building a mutually satisfactory sexual relationship. This book is really about learning and skill development.

The Matter of Willpower

Well in advance of skill development, though, is the matter of willpower. Hundreds of thousands of marriages fall apart before the necessary skills can be developed, because there is inadequate willpower. If a marriage relies forever on willpower, it will eventually become worn out and emaciated. Nevertheless, a marriage short on willpower is vulnerable to extinction when the road gets rocky and the challenges mount.

Willpower and commitment are closely related. Persons tend to have a greater desire to do those things that they have promised to do. If they promised to cherish the other person under every kind of circumstance for as long as they live, and if this promise is current and vital, the likelihood that their spouse will be cherished in a difficult moment is substantially higher.

If I am deeply aware of a particular promise I have made to you, I will try hard to keep it. For instance, if I promise to love you even when we have lost all our money, I will try to love you under the worst of economic conditions. If I find it difficult to love you under those circumstances, I will look for help in learning how to—because I am acutely aware that I *promised* to love you. Promises strengthen my level of willfulness. When I promise to do something, it maximizes the strength of my determination, and I pump up my willpower to its highest level.

If I lack the skill to do what I promised to do, my high level of willpower will make me persevere. And this same willpower will make me search to find resources to increase my skill level. I *will* myself to love you, and I *will* it so much that I will do anything to learn how to make it happen.

Your Current Level of Commitment

One of the chief determinants of marital willpower's strength is the degree to which your promises to your spouse are current—that is, the degree to which you passionately affirm them *today.*

Marriage counselors and psychologists observe that most married persons' awareness of the promises they made at their wedding declines over time. Moreover, the promises they do remember seem less vital and less passionately held as time passes.

The fact is that most persons who enter marriage take their vows in a haphazard, superficial way. They stand in front of a minister, priest, rabbi, or justice of the peace, and they are asked to repeat some words . . . which they do with considerable nervousness. If you asked them a half-hour after the wedding to tell you what they promised, most of them would have only a fuzzy recollection.

That's part of the reason most "older-married people" in our society have little more than a superficial understanding of what they pledged to their mate. I have asked scores of these persons what marital commitment is all about, and they nearly always respond with some form of "stick it out." Of course, that's the *least* important part of the pledge they took. A marriage in which two people are in deep emotional pain but simply stick it out because they promised to is a marriage that will be in deep emotional pain forever.

Sticking it out is worth virtually nothing in a marital crisis, except it gives you an additional chance to make it better. But if all you do the next time is stick it out, your whole marriage will be a series of "sticking it out" experiences, which usually results in a horribly sick marriage. There's no real growth or improvement; it's a matter of muddling through one crisis after another.

The Essence of Commitment

Commitment requires a far more active approach in marriage, and certainly during a time of marital challenge. Staying in a marriage can be totally passive; you don't leave, but you don't do anything to make the marriage better.

The radical part of the commitment vow is that you promise to *love* the other person through every kind of circumstance for as long as you both live. Moreover, you promise to *honor* and *cherish* your mate. Not only that, but you also promise to perform every duty that a husband or wife owes to their spouse as long as you both live. So there are four huge promises that you make to your spouse—all of which are highly active, all of which involve only *your* action, all of which you make unilaterally and unequivocally for as long as you live—no matter what!

Active commitment means that if you are tempted to pick up and run, you yourself block both exits. "I'll tell you what," you say to your spouse, "I'll make you these promises for as long as we both are alive, *and* there is no condition to my promises. If things get really bad, you can depend on me. Furthermore, I will never go out and find a substitute mate."

If married people kept their promises, not only would the divorce rate be obliterated, but marriages would also get significantly better! Show me a marriage in which even one person keeps this pledge with passion, and I'll show you a marriage with a lot of value. Show me a relationship in which both persons keep this pledge, and I'll show you a relationship headed for greatness.

It goes without saying that commitment has become an incredibly cheap concept in our culture. Most married people don't have the foggiest notion of what they have committed themselves to. But worst of all, there is little about the "promises" of marriage that are *current* for most married people. Like one middle-aged man said to me while in the heat of a major marital crisis: "Listen, I took those vows a long time ago, and that's all ancient history."

So what's the solution to this dilemma? First, we have to develop something like "informed consent" when it comes to marriage. We simply must not let any new marriages begin unless the two people really know what they are promising each other. Second, we need to encourage people who are already married to recommit themselves to each other—but only after they have carefully understood *exactly* what the marital promises are all about.

Marital Toughness Requires Continual Fitness

The problems for a marriage in this society are too demanding for out-of-shape marital players to handle. There are so many ways that a marriage can be destroyed; in order for it to be successful, both marriage partners must be highly focused and highly energized. This focus and energy come directly from a keen sense of the promises they have made. These promises must be as current as their breathing.

If these promises have not been burned into their brains, the inevitable problems will roll right over the top of them. Their marriage will be demolished. My experience tells me that a high proportion of married people are totally unfit to face complex marital challenges. Often, they have become flabby from inattention to their original decision—their early commitment. They have done almost nothing *recently* to prepare themselves for the demanding events that are always lurking. They are like tennis players who haven't played for a long time. When they face an opponent who is well-practiced and in peak condition, they get slaughtered. They aren't ready! How come? Because no one warned them to stay tough! Why not? Because everyone, especially the two of them, simply assumed that they could make it fine on the basis of their love, warm feelings, and past successes. This assumption is absurd, but it is responsible for the overpowering of out-of-shape marriage partners by the enormously demanding, but inevitable, problems involved in building a successful marriage.

I am convinced that until we start seeing marriage more realistically, the divorce rate is going to stay at epidemic levels. Marriage is incredibly difficult! We had better start recognizing this. Anyone who is going to succeed in marriage needs determination. Obviously, great skillfulness is required, but the development of the necessary skills often takes time. That's why you need to have a current, deeply owned, thoroughly rehearsed set of promises to your mate. If you don't have this, if you're out of shape, if you aren't ready for a slew of tough battles that will test your strength and your endurance, then you are in danger of becoming a divorce statistic.

Boot Camp for Commitment Training

I take couples into training, preferably before they are disillusioned about how impossible marriage is. If they are reasonably well matched as partners, I am convinced that I can prepare them for the inevitable challenges—and virtually assure them of victory nearly every time they experience a struggle.

How do I do this? Here are the three fundamental sections of the training course.

Section #1: Getting Clear About What to Expect

One of the major causes of marital deterioration is unrealistic expectations of those entering marriage. Nearly one half of all divorces occur within two years of the wedding day. This is a clear indication that people are shocked about what they find marriage to be like.

I try to help those who are entering marriage to expect a relational situation requiring all kinds of change and growth. One analogy I use involves golf. When you pay your green fee, you are admitted to the course. As you stand on the first tee, you are faced with the challenge to hit the ball straight if you are to avoid the trees on the left and the water on the right. But if there were no sand traps, no trees, no water, and no out of bounds, there would be little reason for you to play. Similarly, when you marry, you stand on the first tee, so to speak, and await the action. The very thrill of marriage involves meeting the challenges and improving your game. But the point is that *when* you get married, the obstacles and the dangers are still out in front of you.

The principle challenge of marriage is the weaving together of two complex individual identities and the forming of a corporate identity. The building of a corporate identity, or oneness, is particularly attractive because it offers the potential to meet basic, individual needs in a far more deeply satisfying way than they have ever been met before. But the formation of the corporate identity requires significant flexibility and elasticity on the part of both individuals. Continual negotiation and compromise are essential. If the individual identities are too fragile or too rigid, all of this adaptation will exact too great a price, create too much anxiety, and cause excessive pain. The challenge of building a corporate identity—which requires each partner to make contributions and modifications—is what makes marriage so attractive but so incredibly difficult.

This is exactly where marital toughness comes in. There is plenty of temptation to run, to just consider the whole matter too complex or impossible. But if you're tough, you keep moving ahead. You seek the counsel you need. You stay focused. You don't stop until you're victorious.

These marital problems have a way of staying after you forever. How long two people have been married has some impact on the number of marital challenges they will face, since many issues are worked out over time. But don't fool yourself: As long as two individuals are involved, there will *always* be issues to be addressed. My wife and I have been married for 36 years, and we deal with new or unresolved issues virtually every month. Although we have worked through thousands of issues over the years, our individuality still poses problems for our corporate identity.

The strongest message married people need to hear is that they should expect a significant number of hassles, demands for change, power struggles, and hard-to-deal-with conflicts. The more complex their individual identities, the greater the challenges are likely to be. But at the same time, the more differentiated they are as persons, the greater their potential for weaving together a corporate identity that will be rich with variation, breadth, and satisfaction.

Section #2: Developing a Thorough and Insightful Understanding of the Marital Promises

I have already mentioned that the vast majority of married persons have almost no understanding of what they have promised to their mate. It isn't that their memory is faulty; they simply didn't have a firm grasp of what their vows meant when they originally said them. Making a marriage work, especially during times of severe marital challenge, requires a "promise orientation" that is highly enlightened.

If you analyze the traditional marriage vows, you will discover six separate parts:

1. I will love you as long as we both live.
2. I will cherish you as long as we both live.
3. I will honor you as long as we both live.
4. I will be for you everything that a husband or wife owes to their spouse.
5. I will never give my love to, or get romantically involved with, another person.
6. I will do all five of these things under every kind of condition for as long as we live.

Put another way, I promise to love, honor, and cherish you—and to be entirely responsible in relation to you—under *every* kind of circumstance for as long as we live.

The marriage vow says that if my wife and I don't agree about something, I promise to take her position seriously and to honor her, even in the midst of our disagreement. If I don't get what I think I need from her, I promise not to withhold anything I owe to her, and furthermore, I promise to remain loyal to her. My promises do not mean that I will ignore our differences or fail to stand up for my own thoughts, feelings, and rights, but they do mean that I will never stop loving her and cherishing her, no matter what.

Section #3: Rehearsing the Marital Promises Until They Are Burned into the Brain

The marriage vows are typically spoken during a single occasion under high-anxiety circumstances. Because of this, they frequently have little value in the midst of a marital crisis. Most often, they are about as influential on behavior as a New Year's resolution—nothing more than an idealized wish. New Year's resolutions are usually broken early in the year, often before New Year's Day has been fully celebrated. Moreover, marriage vows seldom have anything like an effective operational plan connected with them.

A few days or a few months after the vows are taken, whatever minimal power they had to influence behavior earlier is usually lost. Because the vows are not repeated over time, their *current* influence on attitude and behavior becomes less and less significant.

That's exactly why I am proposing to change the frequency of the marriage vow. Instead of its being taken once in a lifetime under stressful conditions, I suggest that it needs to be said two to three times a week for the first 10 years of marriage—and at least once a week for the rest of marriage. Why? In order to maintain a steady focus on the promises that form the steel framework of the marriage. With this structure in place, it is much more likely that commitment will shape the attitudes of a person, as well as the behavioral expression of those attitudes. If commitment is verbalized regularly over a long period of time, it takes on enormous power.

When I developed a plan for anger management,[3] I originally asked anger mismanagers to prepare a statement about how they wanted to be the next time they were angry and to read it aloud once a week for 26 weeks. My clients found this extremely beneficial, but when I raised the frequency of reading to three times a week, the effect on behavior was substantially greater. The same is true of marriage vows. The more we say them, the more we will *live* them.

Undoubtedly, challenging marital problems will arise frequently, but the frequency of the problems is not at all our concern. Our concern centers on the way the problems are managed by the two partners. If they approach each problem with an attitude and demeanor best characterized as loving, honoring, and cherishing to the spouse, the marriage is likely to get stronger rather than weaker. But if the two people bring in selfish attitudes, the marriage will be damaged and the problems will remain unresolved. Reciting the marital promises on a frequent basis will insure a maximally fresh and precisely focused set of attitudes.

A Form for Marital-Vow Rehearsal

The most effective way to recite vows on a regular basis is to find a method that makes the process natural, meaningful and even fun. Every couple I have worked with has had their own unique way of managing this task. Let me tell you about one of them.

Sue and Jim came to my office with all kinds of marital difficulties. In fact, they had been separated for a month at the time they called me. We worked through a dozen or more issues over the next few weeks, and they were finally ready to recommit themselves to each other. I suggested the training program I have been describing here.

If you knew Sue and Jim, you would understand how crucial it was for them to stay carefully focused on their promises to each other. Because they both had strong opinions about virtually everything, including each other's behavior, they were constantly in danger of igniting arguments and conflicts. Moreover, their anger-management styles heightened the risk of every interpersonal conflict.

The three of us knew that their vows to love, honor, and cherish each other needed regular expression so that these promises would influence their attitudes and behavior at the moment when marital conflict threatened. When we discussed the need to recite these promises on a regular basis, Sue and Jim came up with a short statement that included every important promise from their marital vows. It went like this: "I will love you when times are good or bad. I will cherish you even if I am upset with you. I will honor you at *all* times. I will never be disloyal to you. And I mean this forever. So help me God."

They didn't leave the house in the morning without saying this to each other. Jim even developed a tune so that he could sing it to Sue. It became a ritual that was full of meaning for both of them. And it had dramatic results. The theme of their lives became "I will love you when times are good or bad." It came to permeate their relationship with each other. It ruled over them even in the middle of their inevitable conflicts. Sue told me many times that the daily verbalization of their promises to each other significantly moderated every disagreement they had.

In fact, exactly one year after beginning this daily promise-making tradition, Jim wrote me a card that said, "Dear Neil, Sue and I are supremely happy together. Everything changed when we began focusing on our promises to each other. We never tire of telling each other what each of us so loves to hear. Sue says to tell you that she has learned a lot of new ways to cherish me while totally disagreeing with me. Love, Jim."

New and Creative Ways to Say Your Vows

"I will love you when times are good or bad. I will cherish you even if I am upset with you. I will honor you at all times." Every couple can profit from saying these simple words to each other every day. The more each person can find new and creative ways to swear this commitment, the better. For instance, some part of it can be put into a lunch sack, engraved inside a bracelet, scribbled on a refrigerator note in the morning, contained in a love letter, or written in the sky above a football game.

The idea is to recite this vow over and over so that when the rocky times come, as they inevitably will, and when the flat places appear, as they inevitably will, the commitment to love, honor, and cherish will trigger new ideas in the brain about how to hold the marriage together.

Periodic rewrites of the commitment statement will make it even stronger. And new ways of living out the commitment—beyond simply verbalizing it—will wind its meaning around the bedrock of your soul.

We are all creatures of habit. Few habits are more crucial than those associated with living out the commitment vows. We want those habits to be so "bulldozer strong" that they will literally overwhelm any opposition.

In the middle of a marital crisis, when an impulse darts across your brain that says "walk out, just get up and leave him," we want the rehearsed response to be "I love you, I will always love you, and I want to find a way to make this work with you." When your brain flashes "gore her with some well-chosen words, make her feel as rotten about herself as you can," we want the steady old voice within to sound loud and strong, "I will find a way to cherish you even in this; this will not drive us apart." Such steadiness and maturity in the face of a momentary thunder-and-lightning storm is only possible if the habituated response is deeply rooted in your being through the long years of rehearsal, well before the rain starts pelting you.

Commitment Multiplies Marital Strength

I have never known of a marriage that didn't benefit dramatically from a simple exercise designed to help both partners clarify and articulate their promises. Couples often call me for help when their marriages are in terrible trouble. Many psychologists and marriage counselors are contacted as a last resort, just before an attorney is called.

Carolyn and Mike were like that. They were fed up with each other! I agreed to see them on a Saturday because they were worn out from fighting, and they were headed to a lawyer on Monday morning to begin divorce proceedings.

Fortunately, they were a perfect case for me—the right ages, the right personal styles, the right backgrounds. Their problems were tough, but we dug in. Together, we began to make some progress, and they agreed to delay calling their attorney. Even though there were huge hurdles to overcome, Mike and Carolyn wanted so much to be married that they worked hard, harder than they ever had, at resolving their differences.

After months of work, their marriage was finally on solid ground. And it still is! They continue to experience times of intense frustration with each other, but now they are deeply immersed in a love that enables them to work through the problems. Like so many couples, Mike and Carolyn crave hearing the other person talk about that special kind of love as they repeat their promises to each other.

I have to tell you that, even today, when I remember one of them finally saying those deep-down, old-fashioned vows to the other, my eyes fill with tears and my throat gets a huge lump in it. I remember how Mike, after all those months of fighting had finally subsided, would look straight at this woman he loved and speak softly: "Carolyn, I will love you when times are good or bad. I will cherish you even if I am upset with you. I will honor you at all times. I will never be disloyal to you. And this is forever. So help me God."

A couple who says this to each other every day is well on their way to a triumphant marriage.

Don't kid yourself. Great marriages are the result of back-breaking work! They simply do not come easily. Two people must be skillful and strong. They need to be tough! Strength and toughness come from reciting over and over: "I will love you when times are good or bad. So help me God."

Maximize the Trust Factor

Spouses in a Solid Relationship
Have Complete Faith in Each Other

"When we were first married, I became aware that I was keeping just a small part of myself from Lee, lest I become too vulnerable. One day, about three or four years into our marriage, I discovered that I fully trusted him, and that withholding was gone."

—a woman from Minnesota

"Trust is absolutely necessary! It allowed me the mental freedom to pursue my role of financial provider without hindrance. To love Betty completely I could not be suspicious of her in any way. Trusting has been easy for me, since we have been totally satisfied with our relationship—no jealousy, no suspicions, and no doubts."

—an 81-year-old man married for 51 years, from Georgia

Hello, my name is Jane, and I attended your seminar in Charlotte. Do you have a minute?"

I had picked up the office phone at eight o'clock one morning, expecting a call from one of my daughters. What I encountered was a woman who sounded frantic.

"I'm in between clients," I told her, "and I'm waiting on an important call from my daughter, but go ahead."

In the next 10 minutes, Jane told me a story that I have heard a thousand times, but she told it so well, and there was so much obvious pain in it for her, that I hung on every word.

"I married my high school sweetheart," she began, "and we have both tried so hard to make our marriage work through the years. I am 36, and he is 37. We've been married for 17 years. We have three children, two older girls and a six-year-old boy. Our marriage has had so many ups and downs that I can't begin to tell you how wonderful and how awful our time together has been. Billy, my husband, has had one job after another since we've been married, and each time he loses one, it's longer until he gets another one. Money has been a terrible problem for us, and the kids and I sometimes have to live with my parents."

Her story was already sad, but then it got worse.

"Billy gets so down on himself when he's out of work," she continued, "that he stays at a local bar until it closes every night. He comes home half drunk, and I think he's started spending time with other women. He tells me, 'Oh, no, I wouldn't do that.' But I can smell a woman's perfume all over him. One day last week I talked him into meeting with our minister. Billy told him a whole pack of lies! He actually tried to blame *me* for what's been going on. He said I'm the one who hasn't lived up to my promise to love him and honor him."

I listened to Jane and offered some suggestions, but it was clear that this couple's marriage was on the road to destruction, all because the trust between them had eroded. Making a marriage really work is difficult under the best of circumstances. When trust begins to dissolve, however, the task becomes significantly harder.

Trust is what enables couples to flourish in the good times and hold together through the bad times. Sudden downturns in a marriage, devastating as they can be, create a crucial choice point for a couple. Their relationship can fall apart entirely, or they can cling to the fact that they have a great marriage and a bright future.

The crucial element is trust. The critical question is whether they can hang on to their deep trust in one another during their times of suffering. It is trust more than anything else that characterizes the emotional environment within which a triumphant marriage can be built. Whatever the economic factors may be, if trust exists at a high level, the potential for marital greatness is strong. If trust disintegrates, considerable energy must be mustered to strengthen it.

Catastrophe Can Cement a Triumphant Marriage

I know a couple, Alan and Linda, who were hit with a devastating one-two punch in a single year. He lost an arm in an auto accident, and then they lost a seven-year-old child to leukemia. They were shocked and virtually paralyzed by Alan's accident, but they were overwhelmed with grief in the loss of their little boy. Tragedies like these would doom many couples, but not Alan and Linda. Despite the excruciating emotional pain that came with these events, they held together and even looked for ways to grow through the terrible circumstances.

This all happened nine years ago, and in retrospect, Alan and Linda say the key to their phenomenal recovery was the direction they turned in relation to each other during the crisis. When the accident occurred, he turned to her *because he trusted her*—and she was always there! She not only took care of him physically, but she also listened and listened some more. The theme of her response was as consistent as day following night: "I would love you just the same if you had no arms at all. Together, we can make it through anything." Little did she know after the February accident that her words would be tested the very next summer.

The diagnosis of their son's leukemia came only 60 days before his death. Alan was still recuperating, and his grief over his son's death threatened to completely shut down his already overtaxed emotional system. Likewise, Linda's grief was almost more than she could bear.

But they turned to each other because they had forged a bond of trust throughout the years. They cried in each other's arms. They cried for days and weeks. Their sobs were like waves beating against the beach. I listened from one session to another as their raw emotions erupted to the surface.

Fortunately, they had called me earlier in the year, just after Alan's accident, and we had a well-established therapeutic relationship before their little boy's diagnosis.

Through it all, they cherished one another. They could care so fully because they trusted so deeply. They leaned on the strong marriage they had built through the years. They also leaned heavily on their faith, which had grown in them since they were young.

If they were your friends today and I asked you to name the healthiest marriage you know, I suspect you would name these two. Why? Because when the rain came in torrents, and the floods rose, and the storm winds beat against their house, it didn't collapse, for it was built upon a solid foundation. That foundation was trust!

Why Is Trust So Crucial?

If the quality of trust in a relationship is more responsible than anything else for the emotional environment within which a brilliant marriage can be built, we must try to understand why. I think I have it figured out.

Two people are at their absolute best with each other if they can be their truest, most authentic selves. When they are being authentic, they are highly consistent relationally, they are creative and innovative, they are generous and giving, and they are free from anxiety. Moreover, being authentic in difficult times ensures a thorough healing within a minimal recovery period. Authenticity is a relational quality that contributes on every hand to the building of a strong and lasting marriage.

When you trust another person, you sense that you can afford to be openly and entirely yourself. That's because trust makes possible the reduction of psychic defensiveness. You don't feel a need to protect yourself from judgment, abandonment, or personal attack. Being free from defensiveness allows each person's central and true self ample opportunity for exposure and expression.

I have discovered that no marriage can be triumphant until both people are able to be fully and freely themselves. No marriage can be maximally satisfying until the central features of both personalities are totally in play. This can happen only when the trust factor is at a high level.

My wife and I have some close friends who are deeply intimate with each other. We admire their level of intimacy every time we are with them. The content of their interactions isn't always positive; after all, intimacy is about the sharing of the innermost thoughts and feelings, and those almost always contain both positive and negative aspects. This couple simply tells each other whatever they think and feel at any given moment.

That's the freedom two persons have when they deeply trust each other. It is the freedom to "be themselves" in the relationship, and this ability is at the heart of intimacy.

This kind of sharing allows two lovers to interweave themselves with each other, to fashion a whole new corporate being, which the Bible refers to as "one flesh." This new partnership can satisfy so many fundamental needs for togetherness—and the wonder of togetherness is that the actualization of two individual selves can be accomplished in the most basic and profound ways. All of this rich and healthy relating happens only within an atmosphere of trust.

When the trust factor in a marriage is at a low level, the individuals' personalities and innermost thoughts—their true selves—remain hidden because the danger of betrayal and hurt is too high. The relationship turns superficial, and the two partners try to be persons they're not, what we call "false selves."

In time, this relationship will become empty for both of them. It hasn't been created out of authentic material. Often a marriage like this will develop a shell that hides the internal emptiness. Both people know that their marriage is just a shell, but they sometimes continue a high-level masquerade because family pressure is so strong. It becomes an elaborate game of "Let's pretend."

This kind of pretense can go on for years. Children can be born into it. The whole family gets drawn into trying to make the shell look as good as possible. But the marital organism, at its core, is rotten, and anyone who is in it or around it will never get fed and nurtured by it. It is decaying toward death, and whatever marital energy that is available usually gets used up in maintaining the shell. But even the shell will in time begin to crack and rot.

Building Solid Trust in a Relationship

When the truth is absent from a relationship for any period of time, the relationship suffers enormously. The absence of truth is as corrosive to a marriage as cancer is to the cells of our bodies.

Before a strong and healthy relationship can be rebuilt between two lovers, the old relational site needs to be cleared. The broken cement of unkept promises must be hauled away. Whatever the lies, deceptions, and betrayals have been, they need to be worked through and eliminated. It is almost impossible to build a great new marriage if the feeling of distrust still lingers for one or both marital partners.

The question of trustworthiness often arises *after* a person has not been trustworthy. I have talked with scores of people who wanted to strategize about how to handle some impulsive violation of their partner—a deception, a broken promise, perhaps an affair.

I'm totally aware, of course, that we all fall dramatically short of being those persons of total virtue that we would like to be. We want to love our spouse more deeply and more fully than any person has ever loved another—at least we feel that yearning now and then. But we sometimes fall far short of our ideal, and we are in the position of trying to figure out how to handle our transgression, this violation of our promises. And sometimes, we would like to handle it without pain and virtually without effort.

When I am working with people in this situation, my goal is to clean up the mess, handle it with wisdom and love, and then get on with the work of building a great marriage. I don't believe in obsessing over mistakes, but neither do I believe in ignoring a serious defect in the structure of the marriage. Not everyone, however, is willing to recognize how carefully damaged trust must be handled and how diligently it must be worked through.

I know a woman—I'll call her Anna—who went back to her home state for the 20th reunion of her high school class. Her husband was not able to go because of an important international business trip, and so she went alone. Anna flew to the event one Friday, and she was nervous all the way. She wondered how she would feel about herself in that crowd of old classmates. Would she sense that she had done enough with her life? How would she be seen by those old friends whose opinions used to mean so much?

To make a long story short, Anna had a wild time . . . in more ways than one. She became the unsure girl of her youth. She drank too much and became far more involved with an old boyfriend than she ever thought possible. Although she didn't sleep with him, she clearly crossed the line of appropriate behavior. She came home with a mixture of excitement and guilt.

Weeks later, Anna still didn't feel comfortable in her relationship with her husband. He was a smart man, and his suspicions ran wild, even wilder than her behavior had been. He became obsessively inquisitive. Anna's anxiety flooded her, and her judgment became dangerously inconsistent. It was about that time that she came to me with two questions: "Should I tell him?" and "What will he think of me?"

This story is so tragically common! Trust gets seriously broken, suspicion becomes obsessive and takes on a life of its own, fearfulness on both sides blocks the road to recovery, and the marriage begins to crumble.

I only wish I could tell you how successfully Anna worked through the serious trust problems with her husband. Unfortunately, though, I saw her only once. I told her that the only way to restore broken trust was through honesty. But her desire to escape unscathed from the event caused her to avoid the confessional process that would have begun the process of rebuilding trust. I never saw Anna again, and I can only imagine that her unwillingness to be truthful has done serious damage to her marriage.

How Do You Start Clearing the Site?

One of the best examples of how to start "clearing the site" happened right in front of me a while back when Emily and Dan came to me for marital therapy. They had been married for 12 tumultuous years, and there wasn't a single six-month period during all those years that truth-telling had been adhered to completely.

"I'm not proud to admit," Dan started, "that I have done some things behind Emily's back, some terribly selfish things I have never told her about—and some things I have." Dan went on talking for 10 or 15 minutes. He detailed rather generally his "deceitful ways."

I listened carefully, and I watched Emily's face. I wasn't sure what she was thinking. Obviously, it had been a long, agonizing 12 years for her, for both of them really.

I turned to Emily and asked her, "Where are you in all of this? How does this make you feel?"

There was a long silence, and then in a soft, close-to-tears voice, she began a soliloquy that must have been building in her for years. "Dan and I have given so much to this marriage . . . for a long time. I love him very much, and I know that he loves me. But for all kinds of reasons, I can't trust him. I want to trust him, but what about all the ways he's deceived me? How am I ever to forget—let alone forgive?" Emily's voice trailed off.

I looked at Dan, and he was looking at the floor. Then I said to Emily, "You're just aching, aren't you? It sounds like you're very confused, that you just don't know how to work through all these violations of your trust."

"You're right, I don't," Emily said quickly. "But we came here today to try to start over. We need your help. We want to make our marriage work, and we know where we have to start. We just don't know how to do it."

I was amazed with the amount of insight they had. What both Dan and

Emily knew was that they had to recover trust if they were ever going to be able to build a healthy marriage. But their trust was so beaten up, so deeply damaged, that they simply didn't know how to regain it.

Clearly, it was crucial for them to start over, and they wanted to. But we needed to clear the site—to deal with all the hurt and betrayal that had damaged their relationship so much.

At this point in my work with them, I recognized how carefully I had to proceed. In the name of helping them "clear away" the old debris, I did not want to create new and needless pain and anguish. If I had asked Dan to "tell everything," to confess it all to Emily, his total openness might have been like a tidal wave. It might have swept their relationship out to sea and drowned what was left of their love.

I told them I wanted to see them separately the next day, and they came right on time. They were excited to get started. I asked to see Dan first.

"Dan," I said, "I want you to tell me *everything* you have done to violate Emily's trust in you. Start at the beginning, and take me through all of it." I asked him to do this for two reasons. First, I wanted Dan to confess everything to someone who would listen to it all and help him gain a clear sense of personal forgiveness. Second, I wanted to assess what we were up against. What part of Dan's situation was the result of character-disorder problems, maybe addictions, and what part of it grew out of a marital relationship that was stuck in a miserable place?

Dan did indeed start at the beginning. He confessed to me about lies he had told Emily in the first year of their marriage. All of the lies were designed to make her think that he was more adequate in his job, more able to earn money, and more sure of his future than he really was. He told me about ways that he had manipulated Emily, ways that he had used her, times that he had knowingly violated her. It was obvious that the playing field of their marriage was strewn with the wreckage of broken trust.

Then I met with Emily. I expected her to tell me how often she had been a victim of all those deceptive and deceitful behaviors of Dan's. She did talk about her hurt in relation to all this. But surprisingly, she also told me how aware she was of her part in the development of the untrustworthy relationship.

"I know that in the early stages of our marriage," she said, "I wanted Dan to be everything my dad had always been in our family. I put enormous pressure on him to produce, to keep our standard of living at the level of our parents, to be sure of himself, to be sensitive in every way to me." Her eyes were full of tears. She was pouring out the guilt that came from a deep and thoughtful analysis of the breakdown of their marriage.

When the three of us met the following week, Dan and Emily shared in general all that they had shared with me more specifically. This sharing was done in a spirit of confession and repentance. They were keenly aware of how they had violated each other and how their early violations had picked up momentum until their marriage was virtually destroyed.

Dan concluded by saying, "I ask you to forgive me for all the ways I fell short of keeping my promises to you. If you will forgive me, I want to renew my promises to you. I promise to be totally truthful in my words and my actions. I want to have another chance to love you deeply and well."

"Dan, I do forgive you," Emily said, looking straight into his eyes and crying like he was. "But I must tell you something that I told Neil. I'm aware that I am responsible for a lot of the mess we got ourselves into. I pressured you, I demanded so much, and I expected you to be more than I had any right to expect. I'm sorry for that. I hope you can forgive me, that you can let me try to correct all that."

Dan and Emily and I were like three washed-out rags when that meeting was over. We had reached down into the most sacred part of human relating. I had watched this couple take full responsibility for their hurtful behavior. They had grieved its effect on each other. Then I had witnessed one of those magnificent, old-fashioned forgiveness ceremonies. Both of them felt the gentle, tender spirit of the other saying, "It's okay. It hurt terribly at the time, but it's okay now. Thank you for loving me enough to take my feelings so seriously. To whatever degree I am able to forgive anyone, I forgive you now."

Thank God! The building site was cleared. We were ready to erect a triumphant marriage that would be grounded in the deepest kind of trust.

The Three Levels of Truthfulness

Tell the truth! It all starts here. A marriage has so much to gain if both partners can rest assured that the truth, the whole truth, and nothing but the truth is the intended goal of every message they give each other.

There are three levels on which truth-telling is crucial. The first is the *verbal* level. The trust of two people for each other can be vitally damaged if truth is not told on the verbal level. There must be no lies! Lies represent verbal violations that have a powerfully negative impact on trust. If she says she didn't buy any clothes, but she did, damage is done to the relationship. If he says he didn't stop on the way home for a drink, but he did, there will be a price to pay. Obviously, the more serious the infraction, the greater the relational price. On the other hand, if two people simply know in their bones and muscles that the other person always tells the truth, the relationship has so much strength to draw on.

Second, truth is crucial on the *behavioral* level. Both marital partners need to become known as people who do what they promise they'll do. If the wife says, "I'll pay the phone bill today," she should pay the phone bill! If the husband says, "I will meet you at First and Main at twelve o'clock sharp," he needs to be there! Trust often gets damaged in a lot of little ways, and if one or both persons consistently fail to do what they say, the relationship is compromised.

Obviously, trust can be damaged in major ways as well. If a spouse gets involved in an extramarital relationship, he or she has stabbed the marriage in the back. Maintaining behavioral truthfulness contributes deeply to the building of a secure marriage.

Finally, it's important to be truthful on the *being* level. This level may never get talked about, and there may never be any behavioral expressions of it, but it will be vital to the health of the developing marriage.

For instance, if a marriage partner pursues inner health, that person will be making a crucial "being" contribution to the relationship. But when that person gets bullied into being something he or she is not, the marriage is sure to suffer. Personal decisions that are made out of timidity and a lack of courage almost always represent a surrender of one's integrity and a commitment to a false self. On the other hand, when a person thoughtlessly allows his or her impulses full expression, with little conscious choice or decision involved, that person is being but a small part of themselves—which is another way to be untrustworthy.

You want to build a triumphant marriage? Maximize the trust factor in your relationship. You wonder how to do this? Tell the truth every chance you get. Talk the truth, behave the truth, and be the truth. If you do this, you will become known as a person of integrity. When your lover relates to you, he or she will know exactly who you are. There will be no need for guessing games. You and your partner can be genuine and authentic, completely free to be your true selves at the deepest and most profound levels.

Five Benefits of Total Trust

Marriages in which two people trust each other at the deepest levels have a least five priceless assets. First, they have emotional insurance that provides support and stability through all the hard times of life. You think this isn't worth much? Ask the people who have been through a few of these difficult periods. Ask them if it mattered much that the person they deeply love was there with them for as long as the down times lasted. My guess is that it mattered more than they can say with mere words.

Second, these married people know that they can go all out in their quest to actualize their potential as individuals. They don't have to worry about failure. If they fail, their companion won't reject them or abandon them. They know they can lean on the unconditional faithfulness of their partner.

Third, they don't have to spend any of their time or energy being suspicious. There isn't any need to second-guess their lover. What this person says to them is truthful. There is total freedom in total trust.

Fourth, they are assured that every investment they make in this partnership will pay dividends. If a man and woman trust each other, they can build together a relationship that will not be subjected to the greatest emotional threat of all—abandonment. They know their marriage will last, so all the effort that goes into making it strong will reap rich rewards.

Finally, they can have genuine peace of mind. When you fully trust your partner, when there is absolutely no need for suspicion of any kind, when abandonment is totally out of the question, you can have one of the greatest prizes in the world: peace of mind. It is the prize for those who are deeply committed to each other for a lifetime, especially for those who have, in words, behavior and being, demonstrated their faithfulness so effectively that the matter is settled. They are each worthy of trust, and they can both bask in the sure knowledge of each other's commitment.

If you are married, I challenge you to maximize the trust factor in your marriage. Take it right to the top. If you do, you will have established the emotional atmosphere in which your most important relationship can grow to its fullest extent. Build a totally trustworthy partnership, and then prepare to move with rocket-like speed to excellence in your marriage.

Tell the truth! Convince your partner that your intention with every message you send is the truth, the whole truth, and nothing but the truth.

Be worthy of trust! In everything you do, make sure that you are loyal and true. If you do, the marriage you have will be grounded in granite. It will be held together by steel. It will last forever. And, best of all, it will allow you to know on this earth that level of love which is woven into God Himself—and it will last throughout the ages.

Get Healthy

A Triumphant Marriage Requires Two Emotionally Healthy People

"I have been through several periods of depression in the last 15 years. I don't understand what sends me into these lows, but I do know I feel totally powerless to change. Dave has been frustrated at times, and I know he feels helpless in dealing with me. But he has been there for me and continues to be."

—a woman from California

"We have had major losses during our marriage, specifically two children who died. When these tragedies occurred, we were emotionally distraught, but our love and respect for each other drew us closer together. As a result, we overcame the weaknesses of emotional health. We learned the meaning of dependency, security, loneliness, 'private time,' emptiness, commitment, and 'hanging in there' . . . our favorite term!"

—a woman from Chicago

Jennifer and Troy came to me for help with their marital problems, but it quickly became obvious that their marriage wasn't the primary issue. Don't get me wrong, their marriage was in deep trouble. They could hardly stand being around each other anymore. In fact, only the impassioned plea of a long-time friend of Troy's to "see someone" resulted in their coming to me instead of consulting Jennifer's cousin—a divorce lawyer.

During our first session, they filled me in on the background of their life together—how they met and why they married. Troy seemed frustrated and angry, so angry that he silently refused to talk for long stretches, as though he felt he couldn't win. He was into withdrawal, and his withdrawal was driving Jennifer wild. Jennifer seemed to fluctuate between attacking and running away. She yelled at Troy two or three times during that first session, and she threatened to leave the office at least twice.

So rancorous was this couple toward each other that bad feelings permeated the room. I could hardly wait to get that session over with. It was abundantly clear that they were stuck, so I decided to see them individually the following week. I was eagerly hoping to discover that we had more to build on than it appeared.

I asked them each to fill out two inventories—the same ones I ask all married persons to complete. One was the Minnesota Multiphasic Personality Inventory (usually referred to as the MMPI), and the other was the ENRICH test. I sent their answer sheets away for scoring and interpretation, and I had the results to share with them individually at their next appointments.

What I discovered from the MMPI was that both of them were suffering from intense emotional problems. Troy's test results indicated that he was alternating between a relatively calm, distant, repressed state some of the time and emotionally explosive episodes other times. He simply didn't know how to handle the hurt, frustration, and fear in his life, and his relationship with Jennifer was the regular cause, as well as the victim, of his out-of-control inner state.

Jennifer's results revealed that her body was a constant voice for the expression of her anxiety. She suffered from stomach problems, headaches, fatigue, and other symptoms for which there were no adequate organic explanations. Moreover, her depression score was sky-high.

Their individual interviews were, I thought, filled with marital scape-goating. All of their individual problems were, in their eyes, caused by their marriage. And, of course, Troy blamed Jennifer for all of their marital problems, and she blamed him. They had come to believe that divorce was the only way they could find happiness.

I met with both of them together at the next session. Combined sessions always require considerable tact, because I tell the truth as I see it about what is wrong with a marriage and what must be done to make it right. It's easy for one or both persons to feel offended, misunderstood, and angry.

I shared with them my observations of all their individual and marital strengths. I let them know how many gifts I believed both of them had. And I made my hope clear to them—that they could find happiness together if they were willing to work hard.

Then I spoke to them as straightforwardly as I knew how: "Jennifer and Troy, each of you has some important individual work to do in order to become emotionally healthy. Right now, both of you think your marriage is the problem, but I'm convinced that it's not. In fact, I believe that if you'll both work hard on your individual lives, you will then be able to build a great marriage together. Clearly, your relationship is painful now, but frankly, that's because both of you have been blaming your marriage for your individual problems. Your relationship is simply incapable of taking care of all these personal issues."

They asked me all kinds of questions about the testing and about my conclusions, and eventually, they came to recognize that they needed individual psychotherapy. I referred Jennifer to a colleague of mine, and I continued to see Troy. They worked hard at dealing with their problems, and after a few months, I began to get a sense of Troy's healing and growth. Moreover, he reported that Jennifer was making substantial changes, too.

Within a few months, the three of us were meeting together again—and then we were ready to deal directly with their marriage. Their individual problems were largely behind them, and they were able to focus all their energy on the future of their life together.

What a difference it makes in a marriage when two people are emotionally healthy. Only then does a triumphant marriage become a real possibility.

Emotional Health and Marital Success

After 30 years of clinical experience, I've come to believe that 75 percent of all divorces involve marriages in which at least one partner is emotionally unhealthy. The marriages never had a chance. Marriages can't cure individual emotional problems.

In fact, when these emotionally hurting people leave one marriage and enter another—often without doing the therapeutic work that is so badly needed—the next marriage becomes the second victim! One of the reasons the divorce rate gets worse with every aborted marriage is because emotionally troubled persons persist in thinking they can get healthy by getting married again. Subsequent marriages, I believe, involve more people who failed the first time because of inadequate individual therapeutic work.

Moreover, there's an unfortunate expectation that permeates our society—that a good marriage will, under virtually all circumstances, make the two individuals involved happy. Believe me, I know marriage can provide profound happiness, but that comes from a loving relationship with your spouse, companionship, support, mutual goals, and so on. The partners don't find happiness just by *being married*. If a person remains unhappy even though married, he or she will often assume the marriage isn't good enough or the spouse isn't the "right one."

In truth, no marriage has a chance of being good unless both partners are serious about dealing with their own internal problems. Psychologists and other mental health providers know that the emotional health of both partners is an absolute necessity if the marriage is to become great. The fact is, I have *never* seen a good, let alone great, marriage where the emotional health of either partner was absent. But why is this the case?

I have spent the better part of my years as a psychologist studying this question, and I've concluded that considerable weight rests with a person's self-concept. All emotional health starts with a solid self-conception. If your positive sense of self allows you the freedom to deal with life fully—that is, to perceive accurately all the facets of your internal and external life—you are well on your way to health. If you also know how to stand in the middle of all these facets and make good, solid decisions that will benefit both your life and your loved one's life, then you are likely to end up very healthy. It all starts with a great self-conception.

Self-Conception Determines Your Style of Marital Relating

When I begin working with a couple in my counseling office, the first thing I want to know is their strategy for feeling good about themselves. I believe the primary motivation for every person on earth is a universal and powerful desire to feel good about himself or herself. From a very early stage in our development, we adopt strategies for bringing this about.

Unfortunately, many of those strategies don't work well within a marriage. Some of them lead to a fiercely independent attitude that leaves the spouse feeling both isolated and lonely. Other strategies maximize dependence, leaving the partner feeling used and smothered. Let me describe three of the most common marital strategies for trying to feel good about yourself.

The first of these we'll call *ownership*. One marital partner conceives that he or she owns the other. If I adopt this strategy in my marriage, my thought processes would sound something like this: Since I own you, I will feel good or bad about myself on the basis of how you look and perform. Because I have so much to gain or lose on the basis of your behavior, I evaluate your every move. I desperately need for you to be at your best all the time. If you perform well, I feel great about myself. But if you fail, my self-esteem takes a nosedive. I certainly don't want you to be authentic if your authenticity gets in the way of my looking good. Because I own you, you may become progressively resentful of me. My strategy makes it difficult for you to be the most important thing you could possibly be—a human being, with strengths, weaknesses, gifts, and flaws.

A second strategy might be called *competitive*. Here, I always have to win to feel good about myself. I need to be stronger, brighter, "righter," more powerful, and more successful than you. It is dangerous for you to take on much power, especially if it competes with my own. My good feelings about myself come with my sense of being *more* than you—in every way.

Obviously, when you are married to a competitor, you are in great danger if you succeed too much at anything. Your partner's self-worth will be threatened, and then he won't feel good about himself or about you.

The third strategy could be called *needy*. In this case, I feel good about myself only when someone is taking care of me. I need to have someone looking out for me, doing virtually everything to insure my security and well-being. I feel good about myself only when my mate is making sure that my every little need is satisfied.

It might feel good to be married to a needy person . . . at least at first. It certainly does make you feel important. But be around a person like this for very long, and you will get sick of it fast. You'll be worn out. When the imbalance in the relationship becomes apparent, it won't be long until resentment replaces the early elation.

The point is that everyone has a strategy for feeling good about him- or herself. Many of these strategies represent a kind of emotional impairment, and when one spouse is emotionally impaired, the marriage is sure to suffer.

Securing a Healthy Self-Conception

So how do you develop a great self-concept? Almost always, that process has a lot to do with the quality of your relationships with your father and mother, or other important figures during your young life. If these crucial people were healthy—kind, nurturing, gentle, respectful, willing to teach, and available to spend plenty of time with you—then you probably emerged in adulthood with a solid internal state of health.

Unfortunately, only a small percentage of people end up with a "natural self-conception" that is strong and healthy. If your current sense of self isn't as positive or balanced as you would like it to be, there are several approaches you can follow to remedy your deficit—most of which are misguided.

Our society stresses the need to *earn* your worth, to produce it out of your own effort. That's why so many people work extremely hard—so that, hopefully, they can feel good about themselves. This strategy results in a lot of productivity, but it seldom results in long-term good feelings about oneself.

In addition, our society teaches that you can feel good about yourself if you are good-looking, wear fashionable clothes, or hang out with beautiful, popular people. So we try hard to play the "good-looking" game. This sells a lot of clothes, hair-coloring products, and expensive cars, but the result is terribly disappointing when it comes to a healthy self-conception. Since a self-concept is internal, external strategies always fall short.

A segment of our society says that we can feel good about ourselves if we are good enough. So we try to be as upstanding, proper, and acceptable as we know how. But this strategy doesn't work any better than the others.

The strategy for acquiring a self-conception that does work is as old as the Bible. It has to do with getting yourself into a right relationship with God. That requires that we let Him be God, and that we get about the task of discovering and being the persons we really are. This strategy stresses that we have been created with great worth and that we don't have to produce more value for ourselves. It is our calling to try to fulfill our enormous potential. When we do this, we discover the excitement and satisfaction that comes from exploring our uniqueness and living it out.

A self-concept based on this strategy is at once authentic and totally positive, and this allows a spouse the freedom to find his or her own authentic self as well. It doesn't have even a hint of ownership, competitiveness, or neediness about it. It doesn't derive its power from productivity, beauty, or behavioral perfection. It is the only self-conception that brings about that kind of emotional health which makes a triumphant marriage possible.

Closely related to a strong sense of self is the concept of authenticity. In my opinion, the key link between emotional health and marital success resides with this concept of authenticity. I doubt that any marriage can thrive for long if one or both partners are not genuine, if their true self is kept hidden. I know for sure that great marriages almost always involve two highly authentic persons.

Authenticity requires that people be deeply and thoroughly aware of all the aspects of their inner and outer lives—thoughts, feelings, needs, external demands, values, and so on. Then they must have both the courage and the know-how to make a conscious set of choices from one moment to the next about how they will think, act, and respond. It is this total attention to *all* the crucial data—and the full acceptance of responsibility for their choices—that determines the degree to which one is truly authentic.

If I am constantly defensive and afraid to reveal my true self to my spouse, then my contribution to the marriage will be extremely limited. I am going to be but a sliver of the real me, and the marriage will suffer from the inadequacy of my involvement. The relationship will be minimized. Both my partner and I will feel the lack of my involvement. The consequent experience will usually be a sense of superficiality and emptiness. Our problem will be that I am only partially present, and both of us will be undernourished.

Similarly, if I desperately try to be what other people want me to be so they will be pleased with me, the marital repercussions will be dramatically different but equally harmful. The earlier emptiness and undernourishment will be replaced by confusion, frustration, and agitation.

Taking Responsibility for Your Emotional Health

Clearly, the institution of marriage is not to blame for the massive number of marriages that end in separation or divorce. The single-most responsible cause of marital breakdown is inadequate individual psychic development and the frantic, misguided search for individual wholeness.

The most crucial discovery that our society must make is that marriage *cannot* provide the basic answers to the individual human dilemma. That dilemma can be managed only when each individual gets personally positioned in relation to both history and eternity. From a psychological point of view, the message of unmerited grace and forgiveness is the only approach to the formation of self-conception that both makes sense and actually works. It results in a self that is woven from the center, from the authentic inner parts of one's true being.

It all starts with understanding that you are worthy of enormous respect just as you are. Then the task is to explore your inner world with intensity and total openness. The goal is to stand in the middle of all the aspects of your life, to choose consciously at every point along the way, and to recognize that the "worthy of enormous respect" dimension is never compromised by either failure or success.

If you are married now, and if your marriage isn't doing as well as you might wish, consider the possibility that you or your spouse (or both of you) may have some emotional health issues that need attention.

One of the most difficult parts of marriage counseling involves giving up the misconception that marriage can solve your problems and make you happy. If happiness requires the elimination of emotional distress, marriage seldom does that for anyone. When it becomes obvious that marital satisfaction is seriously compromised by unresolved individual issues that must be addressed, some people still resist dealing with them. They stubbornly hold to the idea that *marriage* is responsible for their satisfaction.

There needs to be a revolution in North America. We need to take our foot off marriage's neck. We need to point a straight finger at the responsibility individuals have to pursue their own emotional health. If they begin to do this, we will see the divorce rates drop rapidly.

Five Emotional Concerns That Can Cripple a Marriage

I have been asked countless times to outline the emotional health concerns I believe are most responsible for the breakdown of marriages. Let me specify five of them:

1. **Emotional emptiness.** Millions of people across North America suffer from internal emptiness, and that is why they're so desperate for an escape. There are escapes of every kind in our society. The worst of them—such as alcohol, drugs, gambling, pornography—often cause long-term physical or emotional damage to individuals and relationships. Every escape points to the underlying emptiness at the center of the escapee.

   Emotional emptiness is, in my opinion, largely the result of not being intimately acquainted with your inner life. Some persons are far too externally oriented. They're frightened of their own internal world and therefore miss out on the richness and fulfillment that come from examining the depths of who they are. Left with the consequent emptiness, they look for quick fixes for their needs. Unfortunately, so many of these quick-fix solutions give such an immediate "kick" that an addiction develops. The complications of addictions usually sink a marriage, and breaking free from them presents a major challenge.

2. **Low self-esteem.** There are numerous empirical studies that substantiate the correlation between low self-esteem and the negative treatment of others. It is now generally held that we tend to love others to about the same degree that we love ourselves. Therefore, when one marital partner doesn't feel positively about himself, the marriage suffers.

Moreover, a continuing lack of self-esteem often gets blamed on the marriage, as though the marriage is obviously faulty because it doesn't resolve the deficit. If the partner whose self-esteem is strong buys into the idea that the marriage should carry the emotionally hurting person, there will be a sense of unfairness about the gravity of the task. Before long, this sense of unfairness will turn into resentment.

3. **Fear of emotions.** Any person who is the victim of an inadequately structured self-conception may well fear his or her own feelings. Under the influence of this fear, emotions are often repressed. These persons pretend their feelings simply don't exist.

A significant number of women complain that men refuse to communicate on a deep level. My own clinical experience leads me to believe that some men are extremely afraid to face their feelings. They could talk about these feelings, but they fear being submerged by them, literally losing control of them. Their inability to deal with their emotions leaves their spouses frustrated.

4. **Character disorders.** A character disorder is typically the consequence of undersocialization. It is profoundly difficult to build a stable relationship with a person whose character is defective. He or she lies, cheats, cuts corners in every way, and shows disregard for the feelings of others. Our society has more and more of these persons because fewer homes are investing the energy necessary to help a young person develop a strong and durable character.

5. **Anger mismanagement.** More marriages break up because two people don't know how to handle their anger toward one another than because of any other reason. The mismanagement of anger is the single greatest

social problem today. More spouses are physically abused, more children aggressively injured, and more persons verbally attacked because of mismanaged anger than because of any other single cause.

These issues are almost always individual matters and not the result of a defective marriage. There is no question in my mind that all five of these problems can be dealt with successfully. But when they continue to exist within a marriage, tremendous damage ensues. They need to be addressed by the person who suffers from them.

Emotionally Healthy Partners Make a Great Marriage

Recently, I interviewed a couple named Mel and Julie for two hours about their extremely healthy marriage. They're both in their late 40s, and they have been married 26 years. I asked to interview them because three people told me they have a great marriage.

First, let me tell you what the experience was like for me. They invited me to their home, and when I arrived, they were what I would call easy-going, laid-back, and friendly. Clearly, they had been looking forward to my visit, but I sensed they were not at all anxious. It was like they had a story to tell, and if it could help others, they were eager to go along. They didn't seem interested in impressing me. Nor did they seem concerned if their marriage wasn't perfect in every way. I felt totally comfortable in their presence, and I found myself wanting to ask three or four different questions every time it was my turn to talk.

Mel comes from a family of five. He was the second oldest child. He grew up in Milwaukee and lived in the same house all through his growing-up years. His dad was well educated, an electrical engineer, hard-working, somewhat distant, very steady and reliable, not at all flashy. His mother was the emotional leader of the home, a deeply spiritual person who was vitally concerned about each of her children and very involved in their lives. Mel reported that his parents were "quietly in love," and he never doubted for a minute their commitment and devotion to each other.

Julie grew up in California, the youngest of three daughters. Her dad died of a heart attack when she was nine years old, and their traditional family was turned upside down. Her mother went to work outside the home for the first time in her life, and the two older sisters assisted in mothering Julie. Her grandmother also filled in, but her mother purposely chose a job at a cleaners located just three blocks from home. She was always available if there was an emergency.

The loss of her father was a massive blow to Julie. Not only was she unusually close to him, but their family had been a model of nurturing and closeness before his death. There were times when she felt lonely and unsure of herself—especially after her mother went to work. But in high school she became active in a group called Young Life, and her involvement there gave her an important sense of belonging.

Both Mel and Julie were able to attend college. He majored in engineering like his dad, and she pursued a degree that would enable her to teach science-related subjects. The two of them met at a science fair in Chicago, where they had both entered projects. Her project won a first prize, and his received no award. She kids him about that even now.

They were immediately attracted to each other, and they promised to write. They didn't meet again for nearly a year—when he came to California for a job and looked her up. They began to date, and after two years it was clear to both of them that they wanted to spend the rest of their lives together. They were married soon after and settled down in California.

They told me about some tough times in their marriage—difficult experiences that tested them as persons. When I asked them, though, if they had ever had an earth-shaking marital crisis, they couldn't think of any.

"When we got married," Mel told me, "we set out to build a relationship that would be as good as we could make it for both of us."

There was a long pause, and then Julie began to talk slowly: "You asked about tough times in our marriage, and I have to tell you about a major problem we encountered. We discovered that we wouldn't be able to give birth to any children, and when we found this out, we were shocked and terribly upset."

"How did you handle it?" I asked them. "Did you sink into depression? Did your marriage suffer?"

"No," Mel said, "we gave ourselves a while to grieve, and then we began to problem-solve."

"That's what *you* did!" Julie said to her husband. Then she looked directly at me. "It was an *awful* time for me! I think it was all tied up with my dad's early death. I really had to work through all of this in counseling. But Mel was right there for me, and between my counseling, my church friends and my husband, I actually think I came out of all that a much healthier person."

"Oh, she did," Mel said. "She is, without question, the healthiest person I know. And if I was there for her that one time, she has been there for me at least 10 other times. And for each of our kids."

"Your *kids?*" I asked. "I thought you had no kids."

Then with a soft voice, she said, "We didn't give birth to children, but we adopted six babies and raised them to adulthood. We're very proud of each of them."

I was enthralled by their story. Talk about healthy! Before I left that night, I asked three or four additional questions in an effort to find out the source of all that health. It was in response to my very direct questions that they shared some of their secrets.

"For me, it all started in that Young Life club I told you about," Julie said. "I guess I got myself into a right relationship with God. It's a very personal thing for me, but it's been the most important part of my life. My spiritual life is the key."

"Wouldn't you say, Julie, that our spiritual oneness is the key to our marriage?" Mel asked.

"Definitely!" she said.

What an inspirational couple. Their lives had not always been easy, but they had built a thoroughly happy marriage, in large part because they understood the importance of emotional health. It was this health that provided the foundation upon which their individual and collective lives could flourish.

Consistent Qualities of Emotionally Healthy People

What I observed in Mel and Julie is the same set of things I've learned from so many other healthy people. Seven qualities stand out:

1. **They aren't desperate to impress others.** This quality indicates inner security. Healthy people don't buy into the idea that their worth as persons depends on what others think of them. Their inner conviction that they are "worthy of enormous respect" is so deeply established that nothing could shake it. What you think of them or what you say about them is unrelated to what they know to be true. This sets them free, and they experience little anxiety in relation to you.

2. **They don't need to be perfect.** Emotionally healthy people know being healthy doesn't mean being flawless. Few people are even close to perfect. Healthy people recognize how difficult life is and how often they fall short of their own ideals. And they recognize the same for other people.

3. **They are not hesitant about using professional resources in a time of need.** If the situation warrants it, they'll seek help from a psychologist,

pastor, or a respected older person. Healthy people are so secure and confident about their worth that they are totally nondefensive in their pursuit of help. Not only that, but they don't mind telling you about the help they received. Sometimes problems are so pressing that outside assistance is vital, and extremely healthy people take advantage of it.

4. **They don't judge your worth on the basis of external factors.** Healthy people attribute the same worth to you that they claim for themselves. What they know is that you were created worthy of enormous respect, and that's the basis on which they relate to you. That's why you feel good about yourself when you're around a healthy person.

5. **They overcome major problems with even greater solutions.** I keep noticing that healthy people turn tragedy into triumph time after time. Even if the tragedy is momentarily overwhelming, they work at it until they win out. What always amazes me is how they so frequently end up with such magnificent solutions.

6. **They emphasize the spiritual dimension.** Years ago I recognized how many extremely healthy persons have a strong spiritual orientation. These people have a solid foundation that allows them to transcend many of the daily anxieties and focus on deeper truths of life. This isn't to say they don't have problems. They do. But their spiritual understanding allows them to experience inner peace, even in the face of trials.

7. **They reinforce the health of others.** Show me an extremely healthy person, and I'll show you someone who immediately recognizes and reinforces health when they see it in others. That's one of the reasons we all enjoy being around these people. They seem to enjoy pointing out *our* assets. They are free from the need to promote themselves, so they are able to focus on others.

For Emotionally Healthy Partners, the Sky's the Limit

A triumphant marriage is fully possible for two emotionally healthy persons, but a mediocre marriage is barely possible if even one of them suffers from a significant lack of emotional health. That's why emotional health is so crucial. That's also why the time has come for us to start fighting harder for the stability of marriages that are plagued by one or both partners' emotional problems. To ditch these marriages is absurd! The emotional problems are not at all likely to diminish on their own, and the breakup of the marriage carries an enormous penalty for every person involved and for society in general.

The challenge to help create a few hundred thousand healthy marriages in our society is one of the most exciting endeavors I can imagine. When two people form a partnership that is bathed by caring and love, and when they are sufficiently healthy within themselves so that they don't put pressure on the marriage to perform functions for which it is incapable, a fantastic marriage is just around the corner.

Let's go after it! If you are married, set your sights on a triumphant marriage. It all starts with your own emotional health. Get healthy! Until you do, your marriage will be stuck. But when you get healthy, *you will be in line for the greatest marriage you can imagine!*

Work on Chemistry

Maximize Passion and Romance

"After all our years together I can still see him across a room and feel my heart flutter."
—a woman from Washington State

When a marriage involves two people who experience strong chemistry, the relationship has fuel in its tank. If it is headed in the right direction, and if it has a good "guidance system," you can be sure that it will get to where it needs to go.

Having passion and chemistry is vital if you want a triumphant marriage. Good, solid, steady, durable chemistry between two marriage partners is an incredibly valuable asset.

Chemistry makes everything about the marriage work better. When it's present, people get along better, they work together more effectively, and they resolve conflicts with less pain. They not only want to be around one another, they also want to hold hands, sit together in one slightly oversized chair, hug one another, and say all kinds of "sweet nothings" to each other. Indeed, chemistry is fundamental to a great marriage.

I know a couple for whom chemistry seems as natural as falling off a log. Nick and Sarah have been married for more than 20 years, but both say they are as attracted to each other today as they were when they first started dating each other in college. You seldom see either one of them without the other. When the two of them are talking to other people, they're nearly always touching each other—Nick with his arm around her, and Sarah with her arm locked in his. They just plain love being around each other, touching each other, and getting close to each other.

I mentioned my observations to Nick on the golf course one day.

"You and Sarah really seem to enjoy being with one another," I told him. "The chemistry between you must be powerful."

"It really is!" Nick said. "I've *never* met anyone I like being around as much as Sarah. When I'm away from her during the day, I can hardly wait to see her when I get home. And we like doing things together whenever we can. We just never seem to tire of each other."

"That's what I was going to ask you," I said. "You guys have been married a long time. Most people find their attraction for each other waning some over the years. That hasn't happened to you?"

"No," Nick said slowly, "and frankly, I don't think it ever will."

"How can you be so confident?" I asked him. And then he said something that shocked me.

"Because we work on it," he said. "We really work on it."

Did you get that? They *work* on having chemistry for each other. Therein may lie one of the most important and least understood secrets of a triumphant marriage. Chemistry can improve with effort and work.

Can You Create Chemistry?

The idea that "chemistry between two people is either natural or doesn't exist" is so well accepted in our culture that hardly anyone has dared to doubt it. You see evidences everywhere that people see a couple's chemistry as unchangeable—either it's there or it isn't.

I can't tell you how many times through the years I've had people come to me who thought their marriages were over because their chemistry had disappeared. As a matter of fact, the couples usually came only because one partner was devastated and the one whose chemistry had "disappeared" was trying to be kind. This is what these people say: "I just don't love him anymore," or "I don't have any feelings for her anymore," or "Believe me, I've tried. But I'm not attracted to him at all now. I only wish I could be."

What these people are saying is that, obviously, chemistry comes naturally—just like red hair does. If you have it, enjoy it, but if you don't, there's simply nothing you can do about it. Furthermore, they're implying that a marriage without chemistry today is a marriage without chemistry forever . . . and such a marriage is doomed.

Astounding News About Chemistry

Here's the most shocking thing you may read in this entire book: Chemistry between two people is responsive to mental and emotional processes over which we have tremendous control. That's right, you can make chemistry happen. If you don't feel the flutter in your heart for your spouse that you once did, if the magic is gone from your relationship, don't panic. You can change that! I have worked clinically with several couples in an effort to determine whether chemistry can be increased, and the results have been incredibly positive.

Moreover, I have come to believe that most marriages can profit substantially from trying to maximize chemistry. If our theory about increasing chemistry is valid, and if chemistry does as much for a marriage as it seems to, we may have discovered a major resource for improving marriages in North America.

What I can tell you for sure is that I am totally resistant to giving up on a marriage when one or both people complain that "I just don't feel anything" or "The spark is gone." What I want to say is: "Okay, let's get to work so you can feel a lot more than you do! Let's re-ignite that spark!"

When I say something like this, I can almost read the minds of the people to whom I am talking. They think, *You're kidding! Don't try to manipulate me. I know you want to save marriages, but now you're simply going too far.* But I'm not kidding, and I'm not trying to manipulate anyone. I honestly believe that chemistry can be re-created.

Throughout history, chemistry has been thought of as "tricky" and hard to get a handle on. People have always been able to recognize when it's gone, but they haven't had the slightest idea of *why* it's gone. Chemistry has a reputation of coming and going without any logical explanation. For a long time, wise people have known that it is dangerous to build a relationship exclusively on chemistry, because in such cases, when it disappears, the relationship becomes terribly vulnerable to all kinds of danger.

We now have considerably more understanding of chemistry than ever before. While we still have plenty to learn, we do know that without chemistry, a couple's relationship is fragile and vulnerable. We know that chemistry alone is not enough to hold a relationship together over the long term—over rocky ground and flat places. We also know how independent and uncontrollable chemistry sometimes seems to be. But we are beginning to understand how to increase chemistry.

Chemistry Enhancers

Obviously, chemistry and the senses are closely intertwined. For instance, no man or woman is likely to experience chemistry for someone who smells bad . . . or even someone who fails to smell good. Similarly, the fragrance of some perfumes triggers powerful reactions in certain people. I still remember the client who wore a perfume that smelled exactly like roses. Since I love the smell of roses, I looked forward to seeing that client each week, partially because of that wonderful perfume she wore.

I have found that many women are especially sensitive to smell. Some women can tell immediately if there is a new smell in the room. And they respond far more positively to some smells than to others.

Chemistry is often linked to the way another person sounds. The low, sultry voice of certain women is a special turn-on to some men, and the John Wayne voice is uniquely evocative for many women. On the flip side, there is no getting around the fact that some people have voices that are particularly unattractive.

Touch is another sense that enhances chemistry. I still remember the feel of a particular girl's hand when we dated in high school. It had all those qualities of softness that my brain read as "sensual."

Visually, we all have preferences—preferences for certain looks that are especially attractive to us. Some qualities are unusually important, such as a body that is well exercised and in shape. For others, a tanned body is extremely attractive. Some people are drawn to beautiful eyes, while others find a bright smile most appealing.

The bottom line in all this is: Chemistry and the senses are closely linked. Understanding this gives us a substantial amount of control in an arena where control is not easy to develop. Every aspect of the senses ought to be studied and maximized by a couple so that the chemistry between them will remain strong.

In addition to the senses, chemistry is enhanced when our needs are met by someone else. When a person experiences one of his or her fundamental needs being met by another person, they suddenly begin to feel more chemistry toward the "need meeter." Take self-esteem, for instance. We all have a strong need to feel good about ourselves. When we are around someone who makes us feel more positively about ourselves, our chemistry in relation to this person will grow. It doesn't matter much what the need is that gets satisfied; the crucial thing is that a particular individual helps us get this need met. When this happens, the magic begins.

I often encourage married people to figure out exactly what needs their mates have. It's even best to rank them from what you perceive to be most important to the least important.

I am well aware of one of Marylyn's needs. She needs to know that I have thought about her when we are apart. If I demonstrate in some way—any way—that I have thought about her, a happy song plays in her heart. It doesn't really matter what I do; sending her roses probably produces a faster and livelier "happy song," but when I buy her a Mounds candy bar (her favorite) and bring it home, plenty of good music plays for her. From this simple act she knows that I thought about her even when we were apart, and for her, this says a lot about my love for her.

The crucial point is simply this: One way to increase the chemistry of another person is to get organized in your thinking about his or her needs and then to set about meeting them as fully as you know how.

The Source of All Chemistry Is the Human Brain

It was Norman Cousins, one of the most prolific and creative writers of this century, who noted that the human brain is the largest pharmaceutical house in the world. He maintained that no drugstore has nearly as many chemicals, or combinations of chemicals, available as the human brain. If our brains have every chemical that is necessary for producing passion and attraction, we only need to discover the way to signal our brain to release a certain chemical, or set of chemicals, into the bloodstream.

If we are to understand how chemistry can be maximized in a marriage, we must study the human brain. This brain of ours is incredibly powerful—but complex. I talked with a man recently who is the president of a large company. He was talking about computers, a subject on which he is an expert. He said there is evidence that the human "computer"—our brain—has a capacity that is greater than that of the computer currently being used to manage the business affairs of General Electric. However technically correct this assessment, the point he made is monumentally important.

If the capacity of the brain is huge, it seems obvious that an enormous amount of brain activity occurs outside of our awareness. Although we may be consciously unaware of it, this processing may have substantial power over the chemical state of the human organism. Consider all of this in relation to our discussion of how marital attraction occurs.

All of this leads to a theory about brain function, chemistry, and attraction that I believe is revolutionary. You will begin to understand the theory more thoroughly as we move along, but it all boils down to these two points: (1) the degree to which you are attracted to a person depends on what is happening in your brain; and (2) it is possible to program your brain so that you experience chemistry for a person with whom you want to have a great relationship.

At every seminar I conduct for singles, I start my discussion of "the theory" with a description of the following exercise. Imagine that you (a single person) are placed in a room with 25 other singles, all your age and all members of the opposite sex. You are then given three minutes to talk to each of them. When you finish 75 minutes later, I come into the room and take you to a quiet corner. I ask you, "Are there any of these persons with whom you would like to have further involvement?" On the basis of my experience and some research, I would expect you to name three to five of them.

What's dramatic about this is that after only three minutes with each of them, you are eliminating 20 to 22 of these persons who are your age—but of the opposite sex. I always ask, "How did you do that!?"

I reason that you have a highly complex "image" in your brain of the person you would like to marry. As you come to each one of the 25 individuals, you collect information that you compare unconsciously with your internal image, and you get a bottom-line readout. Without your knowing many of the details, your brain sends you messages like: "Move to the next person," or "Ask him another question. I need to get a read on his intelligence level," or "Definitely! This one scores very high!"

In other words, you are being guided through this exercise by a brain that works largely below your level of consciousness, a brain that is intent on matching a preset image with a real person. The process is extremely complex. Many dimensions are analyzed by your brain, and a minimum "score" is preset so you can select the three to five people from the 25 quite rapidly. A massive amount of "computer activity" is occurring for you all through this event.

Sometimes people ask me if I really think all this can go on in just three minutes. I tell them that I believe most people typically perform this complex set of operations in 15 seconds or less.

Then I'm usually asked if I believe that this process results in wise decisions about mate selection. I always answer "No!" I repeat the chilling statistic: "Of all marriages that occur in the United States this year, assuming present trends continue, two-thirds of them will end in separation or divorce." And in virtually every one of this year's weddings, both partners will have received a strong positive conclusion from their brains about the choice of the other person.

There are many possible reasons that our brains sometimes reach faulty conclusions. Perhaps adequate data cannot be collected in such a short time. Maybe too many external and superficial data sources are heavily weighted. Or maybe it's that some people you meet will be too nervous or too defensive to give you complete and accurate information about themselves. But far and away the most crucial reason for the massive amount of invalidity in your brain's readings will be this next concern.

Programming the Brain

On the basis of my clinical experience, I assume that every brain's image of the "right person" is unbelievably complex. That is, there are scores of qualities your brain considers. I call these qualities "dimensions," and my best guess is that some 1,000 dimensions are involved for each of us. In my book *Finding the Love of Your Life*,[1] I proposed 10 basic dimensions including personality, appearance, intelligence, and character. I now think there may be as many as 100 sub-dimensions under each of these 10 more basic ones. The category of appearance, for example, may be broken down under such detailed sub-dimensions as skin coloring, eye color, hair color, height, weight, facial features, and so on.

For each of these, your brain has a "preferred setting" that you like best in another person. It is similar for the approximately 1,000 other dimensions; you have your own setting that dictates your individual preferences. Your brain keeps all these settings straight. Then when you encounter a person, your brain goes into action. It figures the degree to which this real person and your preferred person match on all these dimensions. And your brain will come out with a bottom-line reading. All this in just three minutes . . . or even in 15 seconds.

One other factor needs to be considered. Some of these dimensions are more important to you than others. It is conceivable that you could rank order all 1,000 of them, from that special one that matters most to you, to another dimension that matters very little. It seems reasonable, then, that your bottom-line score will be partially determined by how close the match is between the real person and the preferred person on the dimensions that are most crucial to you.

I know all kinds of people who sometimes sense that they have found the perfect person for them, except for one or two dimensions. I always ask them immediately, "Are these qualities or traits extremely important to you?" If they say they are, I know the bottom-line reading will be compromised dramatically, because there is not a good match on these high-ranked dimensions.

Eventually, we will be able to get all of this more carefully specified so that it will be easily understandable and useful. But even now we can see what an important and complex task your brain engages in. If this is indeed what happens inside your head, we can utilize this information to understand more completely, and modify more appropriately, your brain's output score.

The Origin of Preferred Settings

Nearly everyone asks how our brain got programmed with these preferences in the first place. Most people assume that it all came about by genetics. There has been a strong bias in our culture to believe that chemistry, passion, and romance—three highly related concepts—are uncontrollable, that they exist in whatever form they do because of factors we cannot control, such as genes.

However, it seems far more likely that *learning* plays a vital role in this programming. It may well be that television is the most influential part of that learning. Recent studies indicate that 12th graders have spent nearly twice as much time watching television as they have spent in a classroom. Indeed, television can have a powerful impact when it comes to programming a young brain with regard to important features of the opposite sex.

Of course, there are other powerful influences beyond television. Your relationships with the primary figures in your life, your mother and father in particular, are especially influential. Harville Hendrix, a prominent theorist on this subject, holds that we tend to seek after persons whose characteristics are most like those of the parent with whom we had the least satisfactory relationship. The idea is that we want a chance to "do it over again," and hopefully better the second time.

Our first girlfriends and boyfriends may well play an important role as well. If we had an unusually good or unusually bad experience with the first, or the most important, person we ever dated, we may have been partially "set" in this way. Also, our junior high school friends, both boys and girls, often influence us significantly, because that is a critical developmental stage for the formation of ideal qualities in the opposite sex.

The point is that the preferred settings in our brains are probably determined most powerfully through learning. There is little evidence that we are born with a ready-made set of attractions to certain kinds of people. Hendrix's idea that it comes largely from one source seems untenable in light of our clinical data. It is my belief that we are programmed by many factors in an unusually complex way. And most of these influences are highly untrustworthy because—as in the case of television—they are often driven by advertising. There is almost no reason to believe that the attraction settings in our brains are established on the basis of what would really be best for us.

A New Understanding of Chemistry

If you are married, I hope you are still with me, because this discussion of chemistry relates to married couples as well as singles searching for a mate. I also trust that you have followed the unfolding of my theory to this point. If so, you are ready for the revolutionary part. If this next part is valid, it will change our whole way of thinking about chemistry in marriage.

Here is the central thought I am trying to develop. If your brain has been programmed in regard to your marriage partner, and if that programming has been the result of learning, and if that learning is very untrustworthy, then we need to consider the possibility that you can and should *unlearn* some of those key settings. If you can unlearn those old, unhelpful ideas of what you long for in your mate, then the challenge becomes learning some new settings that will equip you to "turn on" to the person to whom you want to be turned on.

The idea behind all of this is that the preferred settings on the 1,000 dimensions need to come under your conscious control. It simply does not make sense to give this sacred power to the world at large, a world that has demonstrated its overwhelming inability to help us think constructively about marriage, romance, passion, and chemistry.

What I ask married and unmarried people to do is pull all of this information and decision making out of the dark recesses of their unconscious minds. I want them to be able to filter these powerful determinants through their conscious minds, especially in light of their conscious beliefs and values. Furthermore, I want them to focus on choosing new settings for each of the 1,000 dimensions—settings that are much more likely to trigger a powerful chemical reaction when, and only when, they encounter that person of the opposite sex with whom they are well matched.

Obviously, for married people I am looking for a dramatic increase in chemistry in relation to each other. For unmarried people, the time has come for a total re-examination of the process that has led so many people to believe, on the basis of chemistry, that they have found the love of their life, only to recognize later that the chemistry was untrustworthy. It was like their brains sent them a totally inaccurate signal. Their brains released chemicals that turned them on at the wrong time. It was because the settings on the various dimensions were established according to influences that were faulty, if not fraudulent.

A Life-Changing Exercise

I want you to engage in one of the most important exercises of your life. It will take you many hours of hard work, but it may revolutionize your marriage. One man told me recently that this set of exercises took him three full days, but it dramatically changed his marital relationship.

The first task is to locate as many of the dimensions as possible that influence your attraction to others. I have said before that I believe there are approximately 1,000 of these. But you may find that for you there are 500 or 1,500—it doesn't really matter. What does matter is that you bring from unconsciousness into consciousness every dimension you can think of that influences your attraction to the love of your life.

Here's how I suggest you go about this. First, on 10 separate sheets of paper, write down 10 basic dimensions. You can come up with your own or you can use these:

1. Personality
2. Intelligence
3. Appearance
4. Character
5. Spirituality
6. Parenting
7. Background
8. Chemistry
9. Ambition
10. Creativity

Then list as many factors under each of these as you can think of. (Leave plenty of room for writing after each of the factors you list.) For instance, take "Background." Here are 10 general items out of a possible 100 or more that might fall under this category:

1. Family
2. Father
3. Mother
4. Number of siblings
5. Relationship with siblings
6. Extended family
7. Area of country where person grew up
8. Type of church attended, if any
9. Level of education
10. Work history

I could easily increase this list of factors many times over, and this is just one basic area out of 10. Suffice it to say, you want to end up with 10 sheets each filled with as many individual items as possible.

Your Best Estimate of Each of These Dimensions

Once you have as many of these dimensions cataloged as you can come up with, go through your lists and decide—to the best of your ability—what your setting is on each of these dimensions (that is, what you specifically want to be true of the "love of your life" in regard to this particular quality). For instance, take the 10 items I listed under "Background." After "Family," you may put "intact" or "strong parental involvement." After "level of education," you may put "high school graduate" or "undergraduate college degree."

Rank in Order Your 10 Lists

Next, take your 10 lists and rank them according to their importance to you. Read down each of the 10 lists before you do this, and then place a (1) on the top of the most important of the 10 pages, a (2) for the second most important page, and so on.

Select Your 50 Most Important Items

Now select the 50 most important items from all the sheets (not 50 on each sheet, but a total of 50). I suggest you go through all of the sheets and put a check mark by those items that are absolutely crucial to you. If you haven't reached 50 after you have finished reading all 10 pages, go through the pages again. Make sure that you end up with just 50 items.

Locating the "Source" for Each Item

The fifth part of this exercise is to go through all 1,000 (or however many you have) dimensions and specify, to the best of your ability, how you came to adopt the preferred setting you currently have in regard to that dimension.

For example, I have a sister and a niece who were extremely influential during my growing-up years, and I have discovered their active role in my adoption of many preferred attraction settings. It was not until I completed this exercise that I was at all aware of the particular ways they had influenced me. Also, I found that two boys I grew up with had a lot to do with many other settings I have. And my wife has had more to do, by far, with my various dimensional preferences than any other person.

Go through your lists and determine why you ended up especially liking blue eyes, or a quiet rather than outgoing personality, or a strong motivation toward career. I think you will be amazed at the tremendous number of people and events that have influenced you, and you will be shocked at the random way that many of these preferences were chosen.

Now for the Most Important Part of the Exercise

Now it's time to go through your lists again, focusing on each item according to what particular qualities of your partner you think would make you happiest over the long term. Start with your group of 50 checked items. Ask yourself in relation to each of these dimensions what setting makes the very best sense in terms of the overall success of your marriage.

For instance, take intelligence level. It may be that you would like to be married to a brilliant person, but when you stop to think carefully about it, you recognize that a key factor is being married to someone whose intelligence level is roughly equivalent to your own. So what you write after this one is: "Somewhat higher-than-average intelligence, but not stunningly brilliant." Maybe something similar would be written after some of the subpoints in the "Appearance" section.

Compare Your Spouse With Each of Your "Wise" Settings

The last part of this exercise involves going through all your pages and writing a comparison of your "wise" settings (determined by the last step) and what is realistically true of your mate. Let's say that your "wise" setting reads "strong family involvement during childhood." Your comparison statement might read: "John does indeed come from a strong, intact family."

When you get to the "Appearance" page, you may have a sub-category listed as "weight," and your "wise" statement may be: "weight carefully managed; strong discipline." Your comparison statement, however, might be: "John is 35 pounds overweight, and I would like him to have considerably more discipline."

Eventually, you will have several hundred comparison statements, and by simply reading over your list, you and your partner will know exactly where there is room for improvement—where chemistry can improve.

Using Your Lists

You have now completed an extremely important exercise, one which has the potential of revolutionizing your marriage. You and your mate have a massive amount of talking to do. Get some good time together, preferably away from telephones and other potential interruptions. Sit down in a quiet place and talk through this comprehensive exercise.

I probably do not need to point out that this is *potent* material. It has the capacity to do tremendous things for your marriage, but because it is so involved with the intimate and, perhaps, seldom-talked-about parts of your relationship, it has the added potential of creating hurt feelings—and then some anger.

If you think that sharing this information may be too shocking for one of you, don't do it! Let the benefits of the exercise be the personal gains each of you has received and the discoveries you have made. Simply refuse to push all this material on your mate if your relationship is too fragile.

However, glean all you can from your hard work. Especially notice your set of comparison statements. Spend a lot of time considering how differences between your "wise" settings and the actual perceptions of your mate can be harmonized ever more completely.

I have worked with several couples on this exercise, and they have reported to me that all along the way they experienced improvements—sometimes subtle, sometimes dramatic—in their attraction toward their spouse.

Obviously, the most improvement will come if you can understand clearly where each of you is currently falling short of meeting the other person's "wise" settings. You will recognize opportunities to make solid progress on your attraction rating. As you make progress, it should be noted by both of you—and strongly reinforced! If it is, you will find that you can hardly wait to make new changes so that you can receive additional reinforcement.

Believe me, the amount of chemistry in your marriage is not beyond your control. If you take nothing else from this book, I hope you take this: The chemistry between you and your partner can be substantially improved. But you have to work at it—really work at it! I hope you will try, because a marriage with strong chemistry has a great chance of becoming triumphant.

Learn to Talk

Become Masters of Good Communication

"For years we have set aside at least a half-hour each night to talk. Sometimes important things come up, sometimes not. But we know what each other is reading, thinking, worrying about, enjoying, and distressed by. This is a crucial element of our relationship."

—a woman from New York State

"I'm a big-picture communicator, while Carol likes lots of details. I've been, and still am to some degree, a conflict avoider. Carol has been, and still is, more forthright. I grew up a 'pouter.' Carol's mom would not tolerate pouting. We've identified these items and have made major progress on all of them. And despite our differences, we are good communicators."

—a man from Minnesota

Think for a minute about the complexity of marriage. Two unique individuals form a contract with each other. Each of them has an elaborate inner world of thoughts and feelings, goals and dreams, values and opinions, wounds and sensitivities—not to mention a few million needs. These two people say to each other: "I would like to join up with you to see if we can make our combined life significantly more satisfying, meaningful, exciting, fun, full, and loving than either of our individual lives could ever be." Boy, that's a challenge!

So they get together—his two million separate thoughts, feelings, goals, dreams, values, opinions, wounds, sensitivities, and needs, with two million of the same for her. "And they shall be one flesh!" Oh, yeah?! Not without a lot of banging and clanging, conflicting and crying, talking and sharing, merging and blending. Not without a lot of simple, straightforward communication!

Working it out so that "my two million" and "your two million" get along requires an enormous amount of masterful negotiation and adaptation. One flesh, one spirit, one identity, one mission—all that may be the goal, but getting there takes endless, enlightened, gut-wrenching communication!

This matter of communication is universally recognized by professionals and lay people alike as a vital part of any relationship, especially a relationship as intimate and complex as marriage. Consider the following examples of research findings about the critical importance of good communication:

- In a study of almost 500 couples, one researcher determined that marital success is more closely linked to communication skills than to "amount of money" or numerous before-marriage factors. [1]
- Researchers have found significant differences in the communication skills of unsuccessfully married couples and successfully married couples. [2]
- Happily married couples read their partner's nonverbal communication cues far more accurately than do unhappily married couples. [3]
- A Roper poll found that both men and women rated "the ability to talk to each other about feelings" as one of the three most important elements of a good marriage. [4]

It's my conviction that a marriage is about as healthy as the level of communication that transpires within it. It's impossible to imagine a triumphant marriage without two people who have worked hard at mastering the art of give and take. And with every new bit of mastery comes a dramatically increased potential for blending and merging.

I know a couple I would recommend as great communicators. They're one of the 100 extremely healthy couples I studied before writing this book. Because they're such great communicators, they have a dynamic and satisfying marriage.

I asked them not long ago how they came to be such accomplished communicators. "Hard work!" was their immediate answer. As a matter of fact, hard work seems to be the answer we get from couples who have developed mastery in each of the areas our 10 secrets represent.

Of course, this is good news and bad news. The good news is that virtually any couple can learn to master these areas. That provides considerable hope for making marriages dramatically better. But the bad news is that it requires hard work. Hard work is hard! It all boils down to the fact that great marriages seldom come naturally. They are virtually always the result of strong motivation, careful instruction, and endless practice. With this in mind, let's take a close look at the communication process.

Communication Is Simple—But So Hard

Marital communication is simple if you and your spouse know how to do it, if you can do it in the sunshine of a spring day when the two of you agree on everything, if you do it when you're focused on each other, and if you do it when you're rested and peaceful. But communication isn't simple when you're under heavy stress, when you both take a totally different position on some matter, when you grew up communicating deeply in your childhood home but your spouse's family talked only about sports and the weather, when the two of you have communicated about a subject 10 times without resolution, when you talk about an issue that makes the blood boil for both of you. Communication under these circumstances is incredibly difficult!

In essence, communication is just talking and listening. That's all—talking and listening. But the matter becomes decidedly more challenging when the relative amount that you talk and I talk gets raised. What about the pace of our discussion? How long do you get to talk before I do? Who gets to talk the loudest? And when you listen, could you look me in the eye? Why is it that when I talk you seem like a tiger poised to jump in every time I leave a nanosecond between words?

Communication may be just talking and listening, but it sure is hard to do it in a way that both people feel heard, understood, affirmed, and valued. Because not very many people do it right, we have a great scarcity of brilliant marriages in our society today. Listen to this: We could multiply the number of solid, stable, fulfilling marriages by a thousand, or even a hundred thousand, if couples could become proficient at this simple matter of talking and listening.

The Context Needs to Be Right for Productive Communication

Great communication seldom happens in the middle of complexity. A ringing phone can kill the development of a theme. Kids running in and out of the room with their needs and their troubles and their ordinary play can make communication disjointed and superficial. Moreover, great communication seldom takes place when stress is heavy, when neediness is running too high, or when the situation is satiated with demands for quick decisions and emergency measures.

What you and your spouse need is plenty of plain old wonderful time. Quiet, uninterrupted, unhurried, stress-free time. One woman in our survey said: "My spouse and I love to talk together, which is sometimes difficult with children around. We take the time to meet for lunch or get up early in the morning so we can spend some time alone."

If you don't have time to talk, if you always have to put your communication through something equivalent to football's "two-minute drill," you will never develop mastery in this area. To put it more bluntly, a marriage without time to communicate is a marriage headed over a cliff.

There needs to be a healthy context for communication. Maybe you need to take a long walk together, or meet at the park for a picnic lunch together, or take a trip together. The bottom line is simply this: The value of communication and the intimacy gained from it is greatly affected by the context in which it takes place. If that context is characterized by time away from the heavy demands of your routine lives, allowing you to relax and tap into the peaceful, thoughtful parts of yourselves, then your communication—indeed, your entire marriage—is sure to benefit dramatically.

Great Communicators Have Learned How to Talk

We've all had the experience of trying to engage in conversation with a non-talker. Suppose you have lunch with a friend, relative, or colleague, and the discussion goes nowhere because the other person will not or cannot enter into the process. The conversation might go something like this:

You: "How's your new job going?"
Friend: "Oh, fine."
You: "Well, are you enjoying it?"
Friend: "Yeah."
You: "What in particular do you find fulfilling about it?"
Friend: "Hmmm, I dunno."
You: "Okay, anything else you want to share with me?"
Friend: "I guess not."

Is there anything more frustrating than trying to talk with someone who has no clue about how to do it? Extracting information—let alone deeper thoughts and feelings—from these people is like trying to pull an impacted molar with tweezers. If this aggravation exists with acquaintances and colleagues, imagine the exponential increase in frustration that occurs when a marriage partner fails to communicate! There is nothing deadlier to communication than a person who doesn't know how to talk.

In order to know how to talk, you have to know what to say. In order to know what to say, you have to get in touch with those deep-inside-of-you thoughts, feelings, needs, and yearnings. These are the parts of you that must be communicated if you are going to be known—if you are going to be available for merging and blending. If for whatever reason you stay away from all these deep parts of you, the blended relationship will not include the best of you. If it doesn't, it will suffer and so will you.

Admittedly, communicating is not the easiest thing in the world to do. You may think that talking is as automatic as walking, and perhaps that's true when you mean just babbling or rattling on about anything. But talking about things that really matter is comparable to what Fred Astaire and Mikhail Baryshnikov did on the stage. There's beauty and grace to it. And although it may appear smooth and effortless, there's great energy and skill required.

I have discovered four factors that contribute to difficulties in learning to talk well. These range from the somewhat obvious to the more technical.

Reason #1: Low Self-Esteem

If you don't value yourself very highly, you may figure that what you have to say isn't worth sharing with others. You may get to the place where you don't even think about talking. What difference does it make what you say anyway?

There is a high correlation between self-esteem and number of words spoken. That's why some people who are poor communicators need to work first of all on their self-conception, as we discussed in the "Get Healthy" chapter. Until they see that what they say is worthwhile because they as individuals are worthwhile, these people probably won't talk much.

It should be noted that sometimes you will find persons with low self-esteem talking a lot. The words are usually superficial and vacuous, but they certainly fill every square inch of potential conversational space, and, of course, this is the goal. The person's endless verbiage may be acting as a defense so you can't get too close and see what lousy persons they are (or think they are). Or the constant flow of words may be trying to impress you and get you to think more highly of them, but it always comes off as empty. Whatever the case, low self-esteem usually deadens a person about their own insides, and talking from dead insides doesn't add much to communication.

Reason #2: Fear of Criticism and Judgment

Sharing our below-the-surface thoughts and feelings with someone else puts us in a vulnerable position. If you tend to scrutinize everything I say as either smart or dumb, right or wrong, acceptable or unacceptable, then I may quit talking—especially if I am sensitive to your judgment of me.

Of course, sometimes it's just the perception that you're judging me that shuts down my communication, and my perception may be wrong. It's possible that being criticized and judged didn't begin with you at all; maybe that happened with some important figure long before I met you. But because this experience was so hurtful to me, I learned that it's safer to remain silent much of the time. Now my silence affects our relationship.

Painful experiences of constant evaluation often cause persons to develop a highly restrictive communication style. It's not so much that there is nothing to say or that what there is to say isn't of value. It's a learned, protective mechanism designed to minimize exposure and reduce the possibility of criticism and judgment.

Reason #3: Lack of Knowledge About Internal Happenings

In order to know what is "happening" in you, you have to pay attention—you have to look and listen. Unfortunately, the society we live in does everything it can to keep our focus outside ourselves. Examples are television, radio, politics, advertising of all sorts, and on and on. Little significance is given to introspection and meditation.

Many persons in our society virtually never look inside themselves. They never examine what they are really thinking and feeling. They are too afraid of what they might find in there. Perhaps they think of introspection as a sign of weakness. Maybe they think this whole business is pointless or boring. And so they don't do it. They fill every waking minute with external involvement—work, television, radio, newspapers, sports, and play.

That's much of the reason many people have never learned to talk on a deep level. They simply don't know much about what is going on inside of themselves. They may be experts about one or many external things, but they are totally ignorant about themselves.

I frequently lecture about the temptation to avoid the internal. I always point out that there is a rich, exciting, colorful, powerful world inside every one of us. It's not too difficult for most people to learn to access it, but you have to break away from the outside and practice looking inside.

Reason #4: Inability to Put Thoughts and Feelings into Words

Some people don't talk much, but they feel a lot! They just don't know how to put all their thoughts and feelings, needs and yearnings into words, phrases, and sentences. It does require a lot of skill, and most skills require a lot of practice.

I had just come home from playing tennis the other day, and our two oldest daughters, who are both married, were at our house. Three of our grandchildren were with them, and all three of them were feeling as frisky and playful as I was. I turned on a compact disc of march music, with beating drums and blaring trumpets. My grandchildren and I marched all over the house in a straight line, circling around the living room furniture, with me carrying one of them or sometimes having all of them on my back. Now and then, one of them would feel especially happy or sad, or hurt or left out.

Lorrie and Luann, our daughters, were watching all this, and I noticed how they both were teaching those three kids to put their "inner meanings" into words. They kept saying things like:

"Matt, are you just loving that song?"

"You're laughing so hard. It must make you feel good all over."

"That hurt when you fell, didn't it, Marylyn? Are you wanting to tell Grandpa to slow down a little?"

"Joe, are you frustrated because it takes so long for your turn to come?"

Learning to access your inner meanings is a big part of communication. But learning how to put those meanings into words is equally important. Children who learn this skill from their parents are blessed indeed. If you weren't taught by parents, you have to learn some way—with the help of a counselor, trusted friend, or your mate.

It may be that when you first attempt to put your feelings into words you will feel awkward and clumsy. Perhaps someone will laugh at you or demean you in some way, and then you will want to quit trying. But if you quit, what a loss for your marriage! A relationship in which one person has never learned to access and verbalize his deepest meanings is a relationship that is bound to become more and more superficial over time.

Men and Communication

Have you ever wondered why men typically have so much more difficulty talking than most women do—at least talking about deep, meaningful, internal things?

When I think about this question I'm reminded of that hilarious comic strip "Cathy," written and illustrated by Cathy Guisewite. In one of my favorite "episodes," Cathy is sitting with Irving, the frustrating love of her life. Irving is reading the newspaper while Cathy, with arms folded, is looking thoughtful and lonely.

Cathy begins the "discussion" of this common man-woman problem: "We need to talk, Irving."

He looks up from his paper: "We've been talking all day, Cathy."

Cathy is getting more animated now that she has his attention: "But we haven't TALKED talked."

"What do you want to talk about?" Irving asks.

Now Cathy is ready to get into the meat of her argument: "I want you to WANT to talk about things."

Irving is matter-of-fact: "I'll talk about anything."

"I want YOU to be the one to bring the subject up," Cathy says.

"What subject?" Irving asks innocently.

Now Cathy is really getting upset: "US! Irving, the only time we ever talk about us is when I bring it up! I want YOU to bring it up!"

Irving is showing some frustration now: "What about us?"

Cathy can't believe how dense Irving is on this subject: "I want you to bring up things that we need to talk about!"

Irving returns to his innocent expression. "What things?"

Totally exasperated, Cathy gets up and walks away. All she can do is yell one last "AAUGH!"

Irving has stood up from the couch now, holding his paper in his left hand, obviously very hurt and frustrated. He yells to Cathy who is in some other room of the house: "Did all that count as talking, or am I still supposed to come up with something?"

It's true that a man's lack of communication is a real challenge for most relationships. In fact, some current, best-selling books hold that men are naturally action-oriented, while women are naturally feeling-oriented, and this thwarts the communication process. Our survey results lend some backing to this theory. Several men commented on their individual communication problems, and several women mentioned how difficult it is for their men to talk and listen well:

A man from California: *"We communicate well—as equals. But not always. Women are better listeners (at least my wife is). I think that stems from the male mentality. We want to fix things, not listen. I'm still learning to listen, but overall, men tend to talk and listen only to solve a problem."*

Another man from California: *"I did not grow up being open and sharing my feelings. My internal tapes said men don't talk about feelings. Often when Ruth asked how I felt about something, I didn't know how I felt. I could talk about things, but not about gut feelings. Marriage Encounter helped me see that I'm an okay person, and so are feelings. I received the tools to work on communication, and I'm still working on it."*

A woman from Alabama: *"Communication is a weak area in my marriage. Our personality differences account for much of this. I am open and outgoing and up-front. He is deep and reserved and just plain non-talkative. We have adjusted for the most part, but I feel that I have just lowered my expectations as he has not changed in this area (though he thinks he has because I don't complain about it as much!)."*

I need to tell you, though, that after all my years of clinical work, I doubt the validity of the theory that "men are naturally inferior as communicators because they are 'genetically' more action-oriented." Mind you, I'm painfully aware of the problem. I've had literally hundreds of women come for help with their marriage, and a typical complaint goes like this: "Mark just never wants to talk."

Then Mark comes to see me, usually because his wife has told him to . . . or else! When I get to talking to Mark, I usually don't find him reluctant to talk, even about personal things. But I usually find him fairly distant from his internal world—a bit of a stranger to his deeper self. That, I believe, is the crux of the matter. Men tend to be less attuned to their inner messages than women. So a husband and wife will end up circling in different flight patterns.

Why are men less inclined than women to grasp and appreciate their inner worlds? I've done a lot of thinking about this question. My mind often reflects on an event I experienced years ago in Chicago.

It was a Saturday morning, and our neighbor was mowing his front lawn. His three-year-old boy, Jimmy, was riding his tricycle on the front sidewalk. Jimmy fell and hit his knee on the concrete and began to cry. Two big boys—five and six years old—from across the street laughed at Jimmy because he cried.

Jimmy's dad, who maybe had a few fears about his own masculinity, immediately snapped: "Jimmy! Get up from there, and stop that crying! You're not hurt!"

Jimmy eventually stopped crying, but I've always wondered what was going on inside his head. I've sometimes imagined that he was thinking to himself, *Boy, just for a minute there, I thought I really was hurt!*

After hearing "Stop that crying! You're not hurt!" a thousand times, maybe Jimmy began paying less and less attention to what was going on inside of himself. What he learned was that feelings from within which seemed to indicate fragility and vulnerability should be ignored. And the way he ignored those feelings was to ignore his insides altogether. When he stopped paying attention to his insides, he slowly became a stranger to himself. And when he became a stranger to himself, he became less and less adequate as a communicator. He was set up for major marital difficulties.

In my opinion, there has been a "conspiracy" in our society to keep men's attention away from their internal happenings. For one thing, men are asked to be highly skillful in the external world, to be vigilant and protective. This has required a high percentage of their attention. But far more important, our society as a whole has been irrationally fearful of men getting in touch with their soft side, their tender feelings. We haven't wanted our men to be weak, and we have feared that soft, tender, and sensitive men may be weak.

This is one reason we have such a marital epidemic of low-energy, superficial, and defective communication. To make things worse, women sometimes become impatient, and they ask too many questions and fill too many conversational spaces. I can certainly understand their frustration, because a lack of deep communication leaves a marriage hollow and boring. But all of us are going to have to work together to get this problem rectified on a national basis.

I encourage those men who need it to seek 10 sessions of professional counseling designed to put them into closer touch with their internal states and to help them learn to verbalize what they discover. I believe that great marriages must have two great communicators.

Five Ways to Improve Your Communication Immediately

Your marriage will suddenly become more successful if your marital communication begins to change. I have some suggestions about how you can change your communication patterns right away. I suspect that if you give them a try, you will be amazed at your spouse's receptivity.

1. **The next time you see your spouse, ask how her day is going, and then really focus on the answer.** Plan to stay with the subject for five minutes or so. Ask two or three follow-up questions on the basis of her answer to the first question. Show real interest.

   In the past, you may have asked about your spouse's day in passing—just a perfunctory question along the lines of "Did we get any good mail?" So when you zero in on your spouse's response about her day, focusing your whole attention on what is said and the feelings behind it, the change in your behavior will be obvious. And that's great! I remember the first time I did this with Marylyn. She was suspicious of my motivation (Why is he showing so much interest in my day? What's he after?). But I could tell she loved the attention. Over time, she saw that my interest was sincere and that I had no ulterior motives. Then she began to pour out her feelings to me. Our communication took a giant step forward.

2. **When you get together in the evening after a tiring day, turn off the television, put life on "pause," and take some time to refresh your relationship.** The lady from New York who was quoted at the beginning of this chapter has a great idea. She and her husband take a half-hour every evening just to get caught up. It's their way of shutting out the pressures and demands of the world and focusing on each other. Any couple who takes a half-hour every day to check in and discuss anything and everything is going to see dramatic improvement in their communication.

3. **Send a note or gift for no particular reason.** Sometimes communication takes a wonderful turn on the basis of a thoughtful note about something that matters. One of my colleagues told me recently about a book he received in the mail from his wife. It was a book he had been wanting to read for a long time. When he took it out of the package, he saw a letter tucked inside the front cover of the book. In the letter, his wife talked

about her deep appreciation for all the times that he had been there for her over the years. She enumerated several such occasions, and she told him how grateful she was for his faithfulness. He was beside himself with excitement when he told me about this gift. His wife's expression of love in that note meant the world to him, and I could tell that his love for her was overflowing.

All it takes is one rose with a letter, or one candy bar with a short note, or one anything that accompanies a heartfelt message.

4. **Find a way to get the communication flowing.** Some time ago, Marylyn and I began taking long walks (at least for me they're long). We walk about three miles, which gives us time to delve into important subjects. The other night as we walked out of our driveway and down the street, I asked her about her current dreams for her job. Her position is often so demanding that she doesn't take the time to specify her personal goals. She talked slowly at first, but her thoughts and feelings started coming faster as we walked along. I listened and tried hard to understand. I asked questions and then gave her room to formulate her answers. By the time we got back to our driveway, she was still going strong. Both of us had enjoyed every minute of our time together.

So here's my suggestion. Engage in an activity that takes some time, preferably one that involves exercise. Use that time to explore in depth a subject that ordinarily doesn't get addressed. Take responsibility for setting the agenda, and within a few days or weeks, your spouse will begin sharing that responsibility with you. I'm confident that these times will provide you and your lover with wonderful opportunities to communicate deeply.

5. **If there's a crisis for either one of you, make sure you move right in on it.** There is no television program, no business deal, no church event, no anything as important as a crisis affecting your spouse. Marital communication takes advantage of crises.

One of my closest male friends told me about getting a phone call from his wife the other day. Her clothes dryer had caught on fire, and she had been unable to put it out with a fire extinguisher. Fortunately, she was able to get the fire department to come before too much damage was done. Needless to say, she was very stressed. My friend went home and took a long walk with her, letting her pour out her feelings. And they kept walking as long as her feelings kept coming.

When a crisis occurs, it's a perfect time to get close to the one you love most. At such times, thoughts and feelings come to the surface and need to be expressed.

Great Communication Involves Great Listening

Listening seems so easy, but in my experience, very few people know how to listen well. Show me a good listener and I'll show you someone who makes everybody they know better talkers.

I sit for several hours most days listening to people. When I'm at my best as a listener, I exert a lot of highly focused energy. I have to be rested and fresh. If my mind is full of other things—the person I just counseled, the two emergency cases I have going, the article I have to send off later today, a problem in the life of one of our kids or grandkids, or any one of a million other things—my listening ability is seriously compromised.

But when I am on, I am amazed at what happens in people by just listening to them and trying to understand. I have watched people move from total confusion to total clarity—just because I listened to them. I have watched people in the clutches of deep-seated suspicion who suddenly recognized that they were misperceiving the motives of others—just because I listened to them. I have watched marital partners work their way through a complex marital entanglement—just because I listened to them. There is phenomenal power that gets activated because of listening.

You must understand that I am a passionate proponent of listening, and I have been throughout my professional career. I even went to the University of Chicago for my doctoral work in psychology, partially because of that school's Rogerian-based emphasis on careful listening. So if I sound a bit fanatical about listening, at least you understand my enthusiasm.

I believe that virtually every marriage in North America would be several times better if the two people were simply to improve their listening skills. I venture to say that more wonderful moments are experienced in a marriage because two people learn how to really listen to one another than because of any other one thing. Something magical happens inside of most people when they are listened to.

When our youngest daughter, Lindsay, was three years old, she was a blonde-haired firecracker. She had as much explosiveness packed inside her tiny body as the rest of our family combined. I used to notice that when Lindsay and I got into a verbal sparring match, things seemed to escalate negatively as long as I fought it out with her (by the way, if I had a minor edge in verbal skills, she more than made up for it with vocal volume). But one day I decided to try some of my new clinical expertise on her. I got down in a catcher's stance and looked her squarely in the eye. I said, "Okay now, Lindsay, exactly what is it that's bothering you?" I waited for her to talk. There was silence. She gave me a double take, and I imagined that she was wondering what new therapeutic technique was being tried on her this time. But I waited. And when she finally talked, the tone of her voice was different. Her facial expression softened. To everything she said, I just listened and tried to understand. And every time she talked, her voice lowered, and we moved emotionally closer to each other.

What in the world happened? Why did this formerly explosive little girl suddenly change right in front of my eyes? I think the answer is clear. Lindsay was now getting what she wanted. She was being taken seriously. Instead of some giant authority figure who was impersonally "commanding and demanding," I was down there where the level plane of our eyes made us the same age, where my willingness to hear her made her feel important, where she was the only thing that mattered to me in that moment. The listening process worked its magic.

Listening and Empathy

If listening is a vital part of marital communication—and it is—we need to differentiate between listening and empathy. I suspect it is empathy that gives the dialogue of marriage a big lift. Empathy is really about trying to see and experience the world just the way the other person does. In that moment, you put yourself in the position of that other person. You make every effort to understand from his or her viewpoint everything that is said.

A crucial part of the power of empathy is what we call "accurate empathy." This involves our ability to understand so well what the other person is saying that we can repeat it in our own words and have him accept our version as correct. When we accurately understand our marriage partner— and when we do it frequently—our communication skills will carry us rapidly in the direction of a great marriage.

Empathy doesn't come cheap. The first thing it requires of you is a decision that you're going to do it. What you should know is that inaccurate empathy is, according to research findings, more destructive than not listening at all. So, if you're going to listen to your spouse, you need to give all the energy that is required to do it well. You need to really understand what he or she says.

For as long as the encounter lasts, you will need to tune out on yourself. Whatever is on your mind has to be put on hold. During this time, you will need to use all your brain's capacity to understand. Tuning out on yourself is not very easy; sometimes, the matters on your own mind seem pressing and unusually important.

Second, you will have to pay a price for putting your mind into a state of full, activated, receptive alert. It is no easy thing to understand another's messages just the way that person means them. You will need to watch for visual clues and listen for auditory nuances. This takes a lot of focused energy.

Then, in order to find out if you really understand or not, you will need to say what you have heard, to the best of your ability. You may experience severe rejection in this process. The other person might say, "No, that's not the way it is at all. What I said was. . . ." He or she may act like you're a bit dense, or not paying attention, or not trying very hard. This can sting!

Accurate empathy takes a lot of energy, it demands a lot of hard work, and there's some real risk in it. There is nothing easy about trying to understand the complex, inner world of another human being. But it is at the heart of great communication, and great communication is essential for a triumphant marriage.

An Exercise to Jump-Start Your Communication

I can imagine that you are sitting in a quiet place reading this book and that you are yearning for significantly better communication with your spouse. But maybe you've come up with five reasons that it won't happen. Believe me, I have worked with hundreds of couples on their communication skills, and I know how many things can get in the way of progress. Building great communication is difficult.

That's why I'm suggesting you take it slowly and not get discouraged if miracles don't happen overnight. If you can improve your corporate ability to talk and listen just 5 percent over the next month, I guarantee you that we will be on our way to an exciting future.

I've got a simple exercise that will greatly enhance your communication. You and your spouse should pick two half-hour time slots per week to get together just to talk. It's best if these times can be the same each week. Also, get away from the telephone and other potential interruptions. Maybe you can take a walk or a drive.

I recommend that you work on the same exercise for several weeks or months. Spend exactly one half-hour talking and listening. If it seems reasonable to you, take turns starting the sessions. One of you should talk about something that matters to you. Don't talk too long, but address your topic thoroughly. Your partner doesn't get to say anything in response until he has repeated in his own words what you said, and you can say "that's correct." Then it's his turn to respond. This process is continued for the entire half-hour.

Of course, you won't want to start out with the hottest issue currently on your marital plate. But neither do I want you to begin with a matter that neither of you cares about. Somewhere in the middle would be better.

This exercise will improve your communication skills so substantially that you cannot really understand until you try it. Stay at it, too! Don't give it up quickly. Remember, you're only trying for a 5 percent improvement over the entire first month. If you make progress, hope will build in you. And momentum will build, too! You will be on your way.

Communication Will Make Wonderful Moments Possible

I believe that the wonder of marriage involves the sharing of emotions at the deepest levels. This is what first-class communication makes possible. You and the person you love more than anyone in the world can become known to each other so far below the surface that you will never have experienced such intimacy before.

I talked to a large convention of lawyers and spouses in Colorado recently. I focused on the importance of being in a marriage in which passionate feelings and thoughts can be freely communicated on a regular basis. Several couples talked to me afterward, but one couple I will never forget. Our conversation was punctuated with quiet crying and emotion-filled silences.

What this couple shared with me had everything to do with the problems—as well as the wonderful possibilities—of marital communication. They told me a story of their early years of marriage, a story of extremely limited finances, but emotional closeness that left them both feeling deeply loved by each other. Then he became one of America's most prominent trial attorneys, and though she was extremely proud of him, their relationship grew steadily more distant. They got out of the habit of talking to each other, at least about those things that came from their hearts. He was too busy. There were too many other things more crucial for both of them. And as their communication disappeared, their love began to fade. They told me all about that fading love while we stood there together.

What they really wanted to tell me was that my talk had hit them both squarely. Toward the end of my talk, they had passed a note between each other that simply but powerfully indicated their mutual intention to change their communication. They wanted to thank me for helping them to see how crucial communication is to the vitality in any relationship. As they moved away, she said simply: "I think we are headed in the right direction now. In fact, from here we're going for a three-mile walk."

Here's what I know for sure: Any couple who will work hard to talk to each other from their heart and listen to each other with a curiosity born of genuine love, that couple can move at a faster and faster pace toward a triumphant marriage. It boils down to the fact that a loving relationship almost always involves regular sharing. There is nothing in the world that binds two lovers together more effectively than this. It takes willpower to keep it going day after day, but when it becomes habitual, it is the source of virtually everything wonderful in a marriage.

Work It Through

Conflict Is Inevitable,
So Learn to Handle It Productively

"*We try to deal with things as openly and honestly as possible when they first arise so nobody broods, nurtures hurt feelings, or gets resentful. We don't fight—we negotiate.*"

—a woman from New York State

"*We discuss many things and argue quite a bit—especially during times of stress. My wife withdraws, and I increasingly pursue and 'intrude' on her at these times. But we always talk it out, and we resolve our disagreements.*"

—a man from California

I know a couple who fight like cats and dogs, but they are wildly in love with each other. What's more, they have one of the healthiest marriages I know. Does that shock you?

If it does, get ready for some bigger shocks. My years as a psychologist have slowly taught me a difficult-to-believe fact: The amount of conflict in a marriage only determines the speed at which the marriage is moving toward greatness or toward destruction. If you want to sit still in your marriage, rule out all conflict. If you want your marriage to crash and burn, let the conflict rage but refuse to learn the skills necessary for managing it. Well-managed conflict is like a stairway that can lead you to higher and higher levels of marital greatness.

I get nervous when a couple comes to me for premarital counseling and they've never had a single argument. They are complete strangers to a crucial part of married life. They don't have the slightest idea about their combined skillfulness to handle that part of marriage that brings so much potential for positive or negative change.

If any couple thinks they are not going to have disagreements, they are tragically self-deceived and headed for trouble. Almost 50 percent of all divorces take place within two years of the wedding day. Think of that! Couples get married, encounter conflict, and give up—all within two years. There are two points about this scenario that I find disturbing. First, those couples must have been profoundly unaware of how challenging it is to make a marriage work. They were certainly unaware of the number of conflicts that would arise. Second, they must have been alarmingly ill-equipped to handle their conflicts. The management of conflict is a complex but entirely learnable skill. Unfortunately, those couples never developed this skill, at least not to the required level of proficiency.

Let me make this point clearly: Conflict is a necessary part of every marriage for as long as that marriage lasts. If there is no conflict, or if conflict suddenly slows down or levels off, it is a sign that something is wrong with the marriage. There are countless reasons for no conflict, but they all indicate a reduction of that part of a marriage that gives it the potential for growth and change.

A Summary of the Research on Marital Conflict

Scores of empirical studies have been conducted to shed light on the matter of marital conflict and how it should be managed. Let me highlight four of these:

- The largest survey of marital conflict involved 2,143 husbands and wives. The results indicated how negatively many couples handle their conflict. Every year, in 16 percent of American couples, at least one spouse commits a violent act against his or her partner. Further, 28 percent of all couples experience some violence over the course of their marriage. [1]

- Researchers John Gottman and Lowell Krokoff studied 30 couples over three years and concluded that "conflict engagement of a specific kind may be functional for a marriage longitudinally, but conflict that is indicative of defensiveness, stubbornness, and withdrawal (particularly on the part of husbands) may be dysfunctional longitudinally." In other words, if you manage your marital conflict well, your marriage will thrive, but if you manage conflict defensively, your marriage may be wounded for a long time. They also found that men's whining was highly predictive of negative results for both partners. [2]

- In 1982, E.G. Menaghan interviewed 758 spouses and found that discussions about marital differences, though uncomfortable and stressful, were associated with fewer subsequent problems in the relationship. [3]

- In one of the most frequently cited studies of marital conflict, Dr. John Gottman came to a fascinating discovery: "What really separates contented couples from those in marital misery is a healthy balance between their positive and negative feelings and actions toward each other. In our research, we found that in stable marriages there was a very specific ratio that exists between the number of a couple's positive inter-actions—touching, smiling, paying compliments, laughing—and their negative ones. The magic ratio is five to one. In other words, as long as there is five times as much positive feeling and interaction between husband and wife as there is negative, we found that the marriage was likely to be stable. Based solely on this ratio, we were able to predict whether couples were likely to divorce." [4]

Why Is Conflict So Important?

To have a great marriage, there must be two authentic partners. Authenticity involves the full and free expression of each person's true self, with all of its uniqueness. When both people are fully authentic, their complete agreement on everything is highly unlikely. Some conflict is inevitable.

I remember a quote I read 20 or more years ago. Ruth Bell Graham, wife of the renowned evangelist, was asked if she and Billy always agreed on everything. "My goodness, no!" she said. "If we did, there would be no need for one of us."

What Mrs. Graham implied is truly profound. A relationship doesn't need both of its partners if they are exactly the same. The wonderful thing you do for your marriage is to share that part of you that is different from your mate. But as sure as you do share your differences, there is bound to be conflict. This is the kind of healthy conflict, though, that gives you the opportunity to expand your marriage.

Here's an example: If you like country-western music and your partner loves classical, the two of you face a challenge. Every time the subject comes up, you can each deliver a few critical remarks designed to make the other person's musical preference look silly. Or you can hate every moment you have to listen to your mate's music. There's another option, however. You might say something like: "You know, Honey, you love classical music and I love country-western. I suspect that we could come to appreciate each other's musical tastes if we worked at it a little. I would really like to do that. What do you think?" Therein lies a marriage-building strategy designed to expand the boundaries of your corporate lives and to increase the musical-interest range of your relationship.

Imagine a marriage in which one person wants everything about their lives together to be precisely the same. This simply wouldn't be much of a marriage; it would be merely two people living one life. For the person whose uniqueness was ignored and never incorporated, there would inevitably be a sense of not counting much, an intense feeling that his or her ideas, tastes, and preferences were unimportant, unnecessary, and unwanted.

Conversely, a marriage in which each person brings ideas, attitudes, and approaches—even to the point of creating disagreements—is a marriage that will build on the best that both partners have to offer.

The bottom line is this: Conflict that is mismanaged can destroy a marriage. It can turn the whole relationship into a battleground where the only winners are sure to be eventual losers—and the losers are sure to be filled with resentment. If the couple decides to eliminate all conflict in the name of maintaining peace, there will be a terrible price to pay. The individuals' uniqueness is likely to become more and more repressed and stifled. They will have to develop a mask to hide their frustration. This kind of relationship is bound to become cold and distant.

When two people find themselves together for a lifetime—both with an abundance of thoughts, feelings, opinions, and interests—they have a chance to build a magnificent marriage. Blending the uniqueness of one partner with the uniqueness of the other takes great skill, but the potential for a totally new corporate identity with maximum breadth and depth is an incredibly valuable goal to pursue.

Making the Most of Conflict

Couples adopt all kinds of conflict-management styles to deal with their differences. Some are highly successful, whereas others never work. Let me outline three of the most common styles of handling conflict:

Conflict Style #1: Cats and Dogs

This style tends to get the matter resolved quickly, but it may leave one or both spouses battered and bruised (at least emotionally). This is the style characterized by yelling, waving arms, and finger-pointing. It's loud, explosive, and in-your-face.

Jerry and Pat fight like cats and dogs. When they have a conflict, Jerry barks, and Pat hisses. They really go at it! The two of them argue frequently . . . about a lot of issues. One memorable fight took place during last year's holiday season. Jerry's office Christmas party was approaching, and Pat had lined up a baby-sitter three weeks in advance. Unfortunately, at noon on the day of the party, the sitter called to say she was deathly ill with the flu, and there was no way she could sit for them.

So Pat got on the phone and called, by actual count, 17 potential baby-sitters. None was available. She even called two of their neighbors whom they had never used before, but no luck. As the afternoon wore on, Pat was frantic. She called Jerry to relay the bad news.

"It's the sitter," she said. "She's sick and can't watch the kids tonight."

"Well, did you call some others?" he asked.

"Some others?" she said. "I've called all the others. Nobody's available. Looks like you'll have to go to the party by yourself."

"What?! I can't," Jerry said. "You know I'm up for a promotion." His boss had made it clear that this was the big company event of the year, and a lot of expense was put into it. It would look bad if he went by himself. His tension rising, Jerry continued: "Obviously, you don't know what this party means to me! Surely you haven't tried all that hard to find a sitter."

"What do you mean, 'Haven't tried'?" she yelled. "I told you, I tried everybody! Besides, I'm not leaving Tyler and Katy with just anybody. No silly party is worth that!"

"Silly party? Silly party?" Jerry paused to catch his breath. He was preparing to let fly with a verbal barrage, because Pat had discounted his big event.

For the next 15 minutes, the fury raged. It was white-hot, and they made every point they could think of. Finally, Pat hung up on him. She slammed the phone down as hard as she could. Her face was red. She waited for the phone to ring again so she could get right back into it with Jerry. But it didn't ring. Nothing happened for an hour.

During that hour break, both of their brains were lit up with activity. Slowly moving beyond passionately defending their point of view, Jerry and Pat started thinking more clearly.

Driving home, Jerry thought, *It's a bummer that the sitter canceled, but I suppose there's nothing Pat could've done about that. And she did try to find a replacement. I guess she is watching out for the best interests of the kids. She's just in a mess. We'll figure something out.*

Pat's thinking was similar: *Jerry is on the spot, and I know he's got to go to this party. But it makes me so mad when he implies that I'm not doing my part. I don't know how, but we'll find a sitter. I don't want to argue any more. I just want to work it out.*

When Jerry came through the door, their individual brains had them both ready. They looked at each other and both smiled. He opened his arms, and she fell into them. Then they set about trying to solve their problem, both of them throwing out ideas. Finally, Jerry suggested a young couple from church. They were thinking of starting a family and might like a chance to try it out for a night. Both Pat and Jerry felt the young couple could be trusted, and even though they felt awkward asking a favor, Pat made the call. The couple was more than happy to help. Problem solved. The party was a success, and Pat and Jerry were none the worse for wear.

What made this cats-and-dogs approach work for Pat and Jerry? Why did this style, which turns so ugly for many couples, produce a positive result for them? As we will see later in this chapter, this couple did many things right. At the heart of their success, though, was their solid respect for each other. These two moved rapidly into a problem-solving mode because their basic relationship was strong.

Other couples utilizing this approach might be far more negative and hostile toward each other. One partner hanging up the phone on the other might escalate the tension, so that when they met face-to-face, the fight would really get going.

What are the benefits of handling conflict in a cats-and-dogs style? For one thing, all the feelings and thoughts are presented early. Every shred of evidence is introduced through the use of adrenaline-induced energy. There are no secrets; everything is out in the open. The intensity and passion create a tremendous amount of brain activity and verbal expression.

The down side to the approach? Most people do not have a strong enough relationship to handle it. Any mistake is magnified many times because of all the passion involved. With the adrenaline flowing, the partners may resort to name-calling or even bring out old, unresolved issues. For those who don't know how to channel the energy and hot emotions, this style of conflict can get nasty.

Conflict Style #2: Rational and Orderly

With this approach, both partners sit down together and calmly explain their opinions, examine all sides of the issue, dialogue back and forth, and then come to some sort of consensus. There may be tension, but it doesn't escalate into yelling or storming around the house.

Sam and Martha have their share of arguments, but of all my couple friends, they best exemplify the rational-and-orderly approach to conflict. They are both in their early 60s, their children are grown, and they are comfortable with each other—but they haven't always been.

Sam grew up in New York City, in a troubled family where conflict was common. He was close to his mother, but frustrated with his eccentric, untrustworthy father. Sam was assertive and bright and determined to succeed. When he and Martha met, he was a hard-charging young lawyer in the law firm that her father had cofounded.

Martha's upbringing was quite different from Sam's. Her parents were soft-spoken, kind, and seemingly free of conflicts. Martha can't recall ever observing a family fight.

Partly because of the background differences, the first few years of Sam's and Martha's marriage were like a roller-coaster ride. Sam's shoot-from-the-hip style was dominating and, at times, uncontrollable. He seldom exploded and he never threatened his wife in any way, but his conflict style was forceful and potent. In contrast, Martha's approach to disagreements was quiet, gentle, and soft.

Ten years into their marriage, Martha was in a terrible accident. During a snowstorm, the bus she was riding in was broadsided by a speeding train. She spent the next several weeks in the hospital, listed in critical condition. Throughout those agonizing weeks, Sam wouldn't leave her bedside. He prayed passionately for her recovery and channeled all his energy into helping her through.

Martha recovered, and both of them say their relationship changed dramatically because of that brush with death. Sam tells of sitting by his wife's hospital bedside night after night, thinking that she was the best thing that ever happened to him. Recognizing how devastating it would be to lose his beloved, he began for the first time to look seriously at faith issues. He says: "I prayed, I bargained with God, I came face to face with my Lord, and I had a vision of losing my wife that literally shook the emotional ground beneath me."

As Martha regained full strength, she became aware that Sam was a different man. He was considerably more reflective, and his wildness had mellowed. Everything about the way he treated his wife softened—including his style of handling conflict. Coming so close to losing his partner, Sam could no longer shout at her and rant and rave. He felt he was not completely honoring her when he yelled and stepped on what she had to say. He determined thereafter to listen, to sort out their differences in a gentle, compassionate way.

It's not that Sam and Martha don't have conflict anymore. They do. But now they sit down together, state their viewpoints to the best of their ability, and then repeat the other person's opinions until both agree that they're understood. They examine all the alternatives and possible solutions, and they settle on one that they both feel good about. Apparently, this approach doesn't fail them often, because Martha told me recently that she thinks she's the most loved person she knows.

Conflict Style #3: Bury It and Forget It

Sometimes couples will experience a conflict that seems too difficult and too dangerous to talk about. So they will silently agree to leave the conflict alone, to simply let it be.

I have known thousands of couples who have developed a highly consistent style of conflict management. They pretend it doesn't exist! Perhaps they feel ill-equipped to deal with it verbally. Or perhaps they fear their "terrible temper," or their mate's "terrible temper," will get out of control. Whatever the reason, they look the other way when conflict occurs.

When I encounter a couple who have adopted this approach, I am reminded of the 1992 Los Angeles riots. There was a crucial corner in South Central L.A., located at Florence and Normandie. During the early part of the riots, all kinds of trouble happened at that corner, and it was far too dangerous for the police, fire fighters, or anyone else to clear away the debris that began to pile up. Eventually, the corner became impassable; there was just too much junk and rubble in the way.

Some couples end up like this. Their communication channels get clogged, and their love potential is destroyed. By not dealing with their conflicts, their relational progress is blocked. This results in a slow but sure death for the marriage. They don't kill the marriage with vicious fighting; they just let it die of starvation.

A prominent religious couple called me for help some years ago. I refer to them as a "religious couple" because they were both involved in a visible, professional ministry, and this identity, they thought, made open conflict between them unacceptable. So they pretended they had none. I don't recall encountering two people more quietly distant from each other. They could barely stand being in the same room together. They couldn't look each other in the eye. Their unprocessed conflicts were piled so high that there was no way around them. They were stuck in a relationship that was total pretense.

I worked with them for several months before the ice between them began to melt just a little. And, even though they made some progress, this couple never could build a warm, fulfilling marriage. It was one of my most ironic cases. In the name of religion, these two had agreed—consciously or unconsciously—on a set of rigid guidelines that made it impermissible to recognize their conflict. In the quiet brooding of their lives together, they became more and more resentful of each other.

The Consequences of Burying Conflict

When a married couple remains silent about their conflict, they are headed for destruction. Even though there's no screaming and yelling, something is definitely wrong, and it's just a matter of time before the piled up problems take their toll.

Some married couples do learn to limp along with this style for a surprisingly long time. It's usually a case of one of the partners forfeiting their personhood—pretending that he or she doesn't have anything to contribute and swallowing his or her opinions and convictions. Then the other spouse has everything their way. They make all the decisions, and for a while at least, the partners feel good about how their marriage is going. But no marriage will ever be worth much if one person surrenders all of his or her individuality.

Other couples maintain a life together by finding a set of individual interests that takes the focus off their relationship. When a husband gets deeply involved in his business and when a wife becomes totally immersed in her children, the marriage may appear stable—but only because neither partner is focusing on how sick it is.

I have found this to be a consistent trait among marriages: The relationship stops growing and expanding at the point that conflict is no longer processed. If a couple cannot process their differences, they simply can't move forward.

Eight Secrets of Conflict Resolution

The good news is that even the most entrenched conflict avoiders can improve. In fact, even those who are pretty good at settling their differences can make progress and become experts at conflict resolution.

I've come up with eight tips that will help you clear conflict from the road to love. These secrets come primarily from three sources: (1) the 100 healthy couples I surveyed for this book; (2) the thousands of couples I have worked with during my 30 years of clinical practice; and (3) the experience of my 36-year marriage to Marylyn.

1. Recognize Marriage as a "We" Business

I place this secret in the number one position because I've never seen it fail. Any couple who gains a "we" perspective eventually experiences great success in marriage. But a marriage starts to shrivel when it becomes a matter of "two I's."

Of course, this creates some difficulty in the heat of an argument. At such times, it's much easier to focus on what's best for me than what's best for us. It feels great if I win the argument—but it hasn't helped to strengthen the marriage. Start treating marriage as a me-against-her, or me-against-him, proposition, and unity will erode faster than a rain-soaked hillside.

When you give your relationship priority over the two individuals who make it up, conflicts become a challenge that, when handled successfully, will enhance and strengthen your union. No longer a wedge that drives you and your spouse apart, problems approached with a "we" perspective—with an attitude that asks, "How can we benefit from this?"—can be like glue that bonds you together.

2. Process the Data as Quickly as Possible

Even though conflicts can lead to expansion and growth, there's nothing wonderful about prolonged conflict. The secret is to get it out in the open and dealt with. That's why some people who fight like cats and dogs have an advantage. All the important facts and feelings are expressed quickly and unequivocally.

Obviously, I'm not suggesting that you talk over the top of each other, failing to listen and not letting your spouse get a word in edgewise. That violates virtually every important principle of conflict resolution. What I'm suggesting is that you say what's on your mind, that you don't hold back, that you get it off your chest. When everything's out in the open, you can set about the task of merging and blending without the fear of being blindsided by a thought or feeling that one of you held in.

Clearly, we can't always identify everything that's going on inside of us, especially in the heat of a fight. It may take time. But the sooner you can get everything on the table, the sooner you can incorporate all the information into your scheme of resolution.

3. Stick to the Subject

Nothing is quite so frustrating in the middle of a conflict as an emotion-laden comment that is totally unrelated to the subject at hand. Such comments are thoroughly distracting, and they stall any effort to move toward resolution.

I know a couple who constantly breaks this rule. Right in the middle of most every conflict, one of them will throw in some old, unresolved grievance that has nothing to do with the current issue. So why do they want to sabotage the process by changing the subject? Early on, this couple began viewing conflict as competition, and one way to keep from losing involved diversion. They found that throwing in a highly emotional, totally irrelevant comment kept the final verdict from being reached. No verdict, no defeat. Of course, there was never any resolution to the conflict either.

4. Don't Intimidate

When the heat is turned up and things get a little mean, some people become focused on self-preservation. They fear losing part of themselves in the process of hashing out a disagreement. Panic builds, and they start throwing verbal punches. They become obsessed with winning—or at least not losing.

One of the most common weapons in this struggle is intimidation. This is one partner's attempt to make the other person buckle under because of fear. The weapon is threat—physical, emotional, mental. The threat is usually delivered in the form of a loud voice, a dominating physical posture, a barrage of emotional bombshells, or a series of potential consequences if surrender does not occur. Intimidation may result in victory for an individual, but I've never seen it produce victory for the marriage.

5. No Name-Calling

I venture to guess that not a single marital conflict in the history of mankind was ever resolved because one person called the other a derogatory name. It doesn't matter how creative the disparaging label is—if it is meant to depreciate and demean the other party, it isn't going to help overcome the problem.

When the adrenaline is flowing and emotions are hot, you may want nothing more than to pull out that juicy epithet—the one you know will drive your partner wild. Don't do it! Put that name away. In fact, get rid of it altogether. Using it would only result in more hurt feelings, further emotional distance . . . and another thing for you to apologize for later.

Every couple should establish this rule: In the middle of conflict, no matter how heated or intense, there will be no name-calling.

6. Turn Up Your Listening Sensitivity

In the midst of conflict, there is absolutely nothing that produces gains as dramatically as listening. But believe me, I understand that when you're fuming about some intense issue, the last thing you want to do is listen.

I don't know how many times Marylyn and I have laid in bed, each hugging our edge of the mattress, again and again making the case for our own point of view. After repeated attempts to get the other person—the dense other person—to understand our point, one of us finally stumbles onto this key of listening.

"Marylyn," I'll say, sitting upright, "let me see if I understand what you are saying. Do you mean we should. . . . " And then I articulate exactly what she's been saying for the past hour. In a moment or two, I'll swallow my pride and say, "You know, I think you're right. That is a better way."

Why didn't I see the wisdom of her viewpoint before? Because I was too busy defending my own position to truly listen. When I open myself to what my partner is saying, resolution has begun. It works like magic. When you are listened to, you aren't nearly so eager to win at the other person's expense. To be listened to makes you want to listen.

7. Practice Give and Take

Many of us have grown up yearning after, and fighting for, individual attainment. So we enter marriage with a propensity to take. What we must understand is that marriage is a partnership and therefore requires both give and take to be successful.

Some people have learned to give generously and freely, and they seem to have no expectation of getting in return. Show me a marriage in which one person has mastered the art of giving, and I'll show you a marriage in which conflict gets resolved quickly and completely.

I hear your objection: You think I'm overlooking the possibility that great givers will be taken advantage of and walked on. My response is that I've very seldom seen this happen. Far more often, great givers eventually turn their spouse into givers as well. Genuine, gracious giving has a magical effect on the recipient. Only the most cold-hearted person could take advantage of one so loving. When two people develop the capacity to give generously to each other, conflict turns into an opportunity for growth.

8. *Celebrate Every Victory*

Renowned psychologist B. F. Skinner of Harvard University taught us well: Reinforcing the good is a thousand times more effective than punishing the bad. A married couple can take giant steps forward if they will learn how to "high five" each other every time they resolve a conflict.

Why is it that we often fail to recognize our victories? There is something about our society that teaches us to focus on deficits and shortcomings. Seldom are we encouraged to take inventory of our strengths or our progress. When it comes to resolving conflict in marriage, however, it's exhilarating to realize together that a new skill has been advanced. A potential loss has turned into a victory. What an achievement! After the dust has settled and peace is restored, take your lover in your arms and say, "We did it, Honey. We were totally at odds and, yes, it was tense there for a while. But we overcame the hurdle. We jumped right over it! Congratulations. You were great. And I wasn't too bad either!"

Conflict Resolution Is Critical to a Triumphant Marriage

David Olson, who has authored the highly effective marriage inventories PREPARE and ENRICH, has concluded that there are four aspects of a couple's relationship that are especially crucial to the success of their marriage: personality issues, communication, religion, and conflict resolution.

What an incredible boost to a couple's satisfaction when they can blend their unique differences and draw from the strength of their combined contributions.

In summary, it's crucial to remember these five truths:

1. Conflict is inevitable in every marriage.
2. How conflict is handled will determine whether the marriage turns toward decay or toward brilliance.
3. Every couple's conflict resolution strategy must be analyzed in light of their particular relationship.

4. There are eight qualities in conflict resolution that almost always result in success.
5. The greatest of these centers on a recognition that marriage is a "we" business.

Negotiate a Mutually Satisfying Sexual Relationship

A Great Sex Life Builds
Intimacy in Marriage

"Sexual fulfillment within a faithful, loving, supportive, and understanding framework has been foundational for us. It has been important down through the years, and it still is—but not with the same intensity. I remember our wedding night when everything was so new and delightful and intense and relaxing and intense and relaxing and so on. The thought occurred to me that I'd probably die before I was 30 from lack of sleep on the assumption that every night was going to be the same."

—a 75-year-old California man who has been married 51 years

"Another reason I'm sure we were meant for each other is that we are so sexually compatible. As we read books through the years and learned new things, we always explored them. I'm convinced that good lovemaking has been a huge factor in creating harmony and minimizing petty problems in our marriage."

—a woman from California

The most comprehensive sex survey ever conducted in the United States contains one shocking statistic after another.[1] Published in 1994, the results of this survey are so incompatible with what we thought to be true about the sexual behavior of Americans that we can celebrate with happy surprise.

This survey was conducted by a team of highly qualified researchers from The University of Chicago, and 3,342 respondents were each thoroughly interviewed about his or her sexual history. Every part of the study received excruciatingly thoughtful attention, and the results seem unusually trustworthy.

Here are 10 findings from the study that strike me as particularly critical to our thinking:

1. This study found that monogamous couples are significantly happier in their sexual relationships. What a surprise for many people in our society!

2. The data indicate that 88 percent of married people receive great physical pleasure from their sexual relationships, and 85 percent reported the same positive experience in the emotional area. Whoever said that marital sex is bland?

3. There was a strong consensus that extramarital sex is wrong. And 94 percent of all married persons in the survey had only one sexual partner—their spouse—in the last year.

4. A satisfying sex life is not totally dependent on having orgasms. While only 29 percent of women reported always having orgasms during sex, compared to 75 percent of men, the percentage of women and men who find their sex life "extremely" physically and emotionally satisfying is about the same—40 percent.

5. An overwhelming number of Americans are unusually traditional in their sexual habits. For instance, 95 percent of all respondents said they had vaginal intercourse the last time they had sex, and 85 percent said that was the case every time they had sex in the past year. All the talk about a wide variety of sexual predilections of Americans seems totally inaccurate. We are not a nation of people that seeks sexual variety.

6. The study strongly refutes the notion that everyone in the United States is equally at risk for AIDS. The general population simply does not have continuing sexual or needle-sharing contact with the two social groups in which AIDS is most prevalent—gay men living in large cities and intravenous drug users and their partners.

7. However, one in six survey respondents reported having had a sexually transmitted disease at some point. More women than men had been infected, and persons who had engaged in unprotected sex with multiple partners were far more likely to have had such a disease.

8. Twelve percent of the men in the survey and 17 percent of the women reported having been sexually touched by someone older when they were 12 years old or younger. These persons also reported higher levels of sexual dysfunction and general unhappiness.

9. Only 1.4 percent of women and 2.8 percent of men in the survey identified themselves as homosexual or bisexual.

10. The averages for frequency and duration of sex for married couples are amazingly consistent across racial, religious, and educational groups. Both frequency and duration are affected by the age level of the participants, with an average frequency range for number of sexual encounters per month running from four to eight, and an average time duration for each sexual experience running from 15 minutes to more than an hour.

The Importance of Sexuality in Marriage

The 200 persons surveyed for this book reported a broad range of sexual satisfaction. One man said: "Our sexual relationship has been good, but not fully satisfactory. It was best early in our marriage, then not as satisfactory for many years, and now is better again. Sex is not the most important thing in our marriage." Another man said: "I had anticipated our sexual relationship to be a huge part of our marriage. It is important, but not nearly as important as I expected, and far less important than many other things." It seems clear that some highly successful marriages do not include a sexual component that is totally satisfying.

Other persons talked about improvement in sexual satisfaction over the course of their marriage and the many benefits that accrue from this change. One lady said: "We were both somewhat inhibited initially, and it was some time before I was able to communicate my needs. Our sexual relationship is great now—and a very important part of our marriage."

While it seems clear that a mutually satisfying sexual relationship enhances every marriage, it is equally clear that great marriages can often be fashioned without great sex. But there's little doubt that if great sex for both partners can be obtained, it will contribute substantially to the management of marital stress and the attainment of marital goals.

Dr. Clifford and Joyce Penner have been my partners in the practice of psychology for nearly 27 years. They have written six excellent books about sexual adjustment in marriage, the most famous being the best-selling *The Gift of Sex*.[2] I interviewed them for several hours in preparation for writing this chapter. I began with this question: "What percentage of couples can attain a mutually satisfying sexual relationship?" I was startled when they both answered at the same time with the same answer: "100 percent of them." When I pressed them, Cliff said, "We've never worked with a single married couple whom we felt were incapable of attaining a high level of sexual satisfaction with each other."

"Amazing!" I said. "How many of these couples attain this kind of mutual satisfaction quite naturally, without having to really work at it?"

"About one-third of them," Joyce replied.

Over the next few hours, I asked the Penners every question I could think of about how the "other two-thirds" of all married couples can reach the high level of sexual satisfaction that so greatly facilitates the building of a triumphant marriage. Their answers were straightforward, clear, and simple.

Ten Crucial Factors for a Great Sex Life

I asked the Penners for their list of recommendations for any couple who wants to have a mutually satisfying sexual relationship. After 25 years of holding seminars throughout North America, working with thousands of couples on their sexual relationship, appearing on hundreds of radio and television talk shows, and writing all these books about great sex in marriage, the Penners came at my question with tremendous enthusiasm and confidence. Here are the 10 recommendations they have for how to create a great sex life:

1. **The most vital factor in producing a great sexual relationship in marriage revolves around the role of the man.** The Penners have found that sexual patterns in a marriage begin to change dramatically when the man changes, even when the woman may be the one hindering a vital sexual relationship. So even though "it takes two to tango," as they say, the greater responsibility for improvement rests with the husband.

2. **The man must move in the direction of the woman's needs.** He needs to become acutely aware of as many of her spiritual and emotional needs as he possibly can. His awareness, obviously, will increase in direct proportion to his ability to listen to her.

3. **The woman needs to learn how to *take*.** She needs to listen carefully to her body, and then seek what will satisfy her desires. Though wives are typically eager to please their husbands, they should be ready to receive an equal degree of pleasure.

4. **The woman must feel free to lead in the sexual experience.** The Penners quoted an Old Testament passage from the Song of Solomon that teaches a three-step process that leads to dramatic sexual improvement. First, the man affirms the woman; he talks freely about her virtues. Second, the woman takes the lead; she proceeds at her speed, and she lets the man know her thoughts and desires at all times. Third, the man responds; he listens carefully to what she says, and he acts only in response to her desires. (The most common example is that women stop kissing passionately because the man always wants more. If women want to kiss for an hour and that's all, men should accommodate that wish.)

5. **The man must progress very s-l-o-w-l-y.** The previous point was so important that the Penners underlined it by saying, "The man must slow way down." They referred to the song by the Pointer Sisters about "the man with the slow hands." The image that represents the best relative pace for the two persons involves a man and woman riding their separate bicycles down the road. The woman is slightly in the lead, and the man rides with his front wheel just behind her front wheel. He isn't far behind, but he lets her take the lead.

6. **The man needs to remain flexible, without a set "agenda" for how things are supposed to go.** His "guidance system" should be his wife. Many men try to get the recipe down and then follow it. This almost never works because a woman's sexual desires, needs, and responses cannot be predicted from one time to the next.

7. **Both husband and wife need to be into the sexual process for the pleasure of it—not for the result of it.** The goal of sex is to build intimacy with your spouse. The secret is to enjoy both your own body and your partner's. If climax is not reached for either partner, it shouldn't be seen as a big disappointment or failure.

8. **If one of the partners was the victim of sexual abuse during childhood, there must be healing from the trauma.** The victims of abuse often carry into marriage emotional scars that hinder free and uninhibited sexual expression. (And understand that they are the victims. I have the utmost compassion for those who have suffered abuse.) Most often this healing process requires a professional to help you face the abuse, grieve the losses involved, and regain a sense of wholeness. In addition, support groups and books are readily available to help you through this process. (The University of Chicago study stated that 17 percent of women are abused during childhood. However, after years of clinical research, the Penners believe that number is actually closer to 35 percent.)

9. **Mutual satisfaction is the expectation in every sexual experience.** The woman must be able to allow an orgasm if she wants one. The fundamental requirement for satisfaction, however, is a deep sense of interpersonal closeness and warmth.

10. **It is vital that both partners know how the body works sexually.** Don't laugh! Most people enter marriage with many misconceptions about how things work. A thorough understanding will make expectations far more reasonable, and couples won't suffer from the disappointment and disillusionment that come from unrealistic desires and demands.

   I want to make it clear that mutual sexual satisfaction is a goal that every couple should pursue with great enthusiasm. If all couples in North America could spend a few hours with highly competent sexual therapists like the Penners, their marriages would experience a dramatic improvement in this area. If you need guidance along the way to help make your sex life deeply satisfying, I encourage you to look for professionals who are emotionally healthy themselves, and who have the ability to help couples merge physical technique and spiritual sensitivity into a totally delightful sexual experience. If there are no sexual counselors in your area, I encourage you to buy a good book on marital sex, read it with your spouse, and keep working on the development of your sexual relationship.

Sexual Satisfaction as an Index of Relational Health

My clinical experience has taught me that the relationship between marital health and sexual satisfaction is a very complex one. For instance, I have worked with some couples whose overall compatibility ratio is very low, but their sexual satisfaction level is unusually high. I have had some couples who simply couldn't get along, and they separated, but they continued seeing each other frequently to have sex. I have worked with other couples who virtually hated each other, but they didn't separate because they couldn't imagine giving up something as vital to them as their sexual relationship. One couple actually told me that they both keep their eyes tightly closed during sex because, as good as the sex is, they can't stand even the thought of being with each other, let alone making love to each other.

On the other hand, I have seen scores of couples through the years who felt they didn't have a very satisfying sexual relationship but loved each other deeply. Many of these couples would never consider leaving the marriage; in fact, they might very well rate their marriage as extremely satisfying.

There is little doubt in my mind that when all other factors are positive for a couple, the lack of a good sexual relationship will seldom sink the marriage. Sex is usually not vital enough to devastate any marriage all by itself—if other factors are sufficiently positive. But I must tell you that I have never seen what I call a triumphant marriage in which the sexual relationship was disappointing. And even though I mentioned earlier about the way that some couples stay together (or get together periodically) for the sex even though their relationship is worse than mediocre, the fact is that a great sexual relationship enhances most marriages in a significant way.

I believe that if we could teach every couple in North America to improve their sexual relationship by just 10 percent, we could lower the divorce rate by more than 10 percent. Further, we could increase the marital satisfaction rate enormously. Why? Because every couple in America would suddenly have a sexual relationship that's 10 percent better, and even more important, every couple would have a sense of hope. It's hope that brings about an acceleration of marital growth. The hope rests on the fact that if we can get a 10 percent improvement rate for every couple, then why can't we get a 15 percent improvement rate? When improvement becomes possible on the basis of factors over which we have control, we begin to sense that there may be incredible gains available to those couples who want to work hard at it.

Sexual Problems in Marriage: Three Case Studies

In order to illustrate the various types of sexual problems in marriage— and how to proceed with them—I want to tell you about three actual cases.

Case Study #1: Laurel and Steve
Laurel, a 29-year-old mother of two sons, called me about her marriage.

She and Steve, 32, had been married seven years and had tried two other counselors, but Steve always found an excuse for not attending after a couple of sessions. I set up an appointment to see them the next day.

They came together, and I escorted them in from the waiting room right on time. Laurel was eager to talk, and she would have dominated the conversation if I hadn't continued to make plenty of conversational space for Steve. What became obvious early on was that Laurel was filled with concern about her marriage. She was frightened that it was falling apart, and she felt totally helpless to change it. The more her anxiety motivated her to talk, the more Steve—like a turtle—pulled his head in under his thick shell.

I perceived that Laurel was reasonably happy, stable, and emotionally secure. The problems didn't seem to belong to her. The only thing I needed to do with her was to calm her down and get her to back off. She kept us from focusing squarely on Steve's problem because her nervous chatter kept getting in the way.

The superficial description of their problem went like this: The relationship seemed fine during the courtship and for the first two years of marriage, but after their first son was born, sex between them became more and more infrequent and unsatisfying. Their current sexual relationship was almost nonexistent. From Laurel's point of view, Steve had totally withdrawn from her. When this withdrawal had started several years earlier, Laurel had tried everything. For several months, she attempted to reason with him, but this usually led to even greater distancing. Then she tried to woo him with flashier clothes, carefully planned meals, and weekends away. Despite her efforts, nothing seemed to draw Steve back into the relationship.

I suggested individual appointments early in the next week. I was especially interested in seeing Steve, because I had become more and more convinced that the problem was with him.

I'm certainly not always right, but this time I was. The hour with Steve was filled with stories about his early life that moved like a heat-seeking missile to his relationship with his stepfather. In one of those heart-breaking revelations, he told me how his stepfather had sexually violated him when Steve was only 11 years old. The abuse had continued for four years, and every time Steve was in the house and his mother was at work, Steve became vulnerable to this man's pathological domination.

"Have you ever shared this with Laurel?" I asked.

"No."

"May I ask you why not?"

Staring at the floor, he replied quietly that he was too ashamed.

I then asked, "What about the two other therapists you saw? Did you tell them?"

"No," he said. "I never saw them alone. I was always with Laurel."

He did say, though, that he desperately wanted to deal with the issue, because he saw how it was damaging his marriage. Nevertheless, he still wasn't ready to tell Laurel about it.

"Okay," I said, "I want to see you twice a week so that we can get to work on this severe psychic injury." Steve agreed in an instant. I worked it out with Laurel so that I could see Steve alone without raising her suspicion too much.

He never missed a session, and he was not late once. His sexual problems persisted, but in time we worked through the hurt, fear, guilt, shame, and sexual identity confusion he experienced. After several months, we brought Laurel in, and Steve was able to tell her everything. While our progress was something like two-steps-forward-one-step-back, it was positive enough that within a few months, Steve and Laurel began feeling substantially closer to each other. Little gains turned into slightly bigger ones, and eventually, they were far along the road to recovery.

Sometimes, in cases like this one, the sexual problem is not a marital problem at all. In a world in which children are often victims of horrible crimes, the result is frequently a kind of brokenness that shows itself wherever relational intimacy is most intense. What we have to guard against in cases like this one is that the marriage doesn't get blamed.

There was no way that Steve and Laurel could ever have had a decent sexual relationship until Steve had a chance to heal. Laurel's nature was to confront the problem, to take the blame if she needed to, and to take as much control of the situation as she could. All her efforts in this regard only made things worse. The more she pursued Steve, the more he ran away to protect his secret. Thank God for the individual time I had with Steve that allowed him to share the truth. This lit the path we needed to follow to help him recover—and to give his marriage a wonderful future.

Case Study #2: Jim and Erin

Jim told me during our first session that "his marriage had gone flat." Nothing was seriously wrong, but nothing was right either. Sex for him and Erin was infrequent, and he was frustrated by how blasé their marriage had become.

When I saw them together for the first time, Jim did 75 percent of the talking. Erin spoke only when I asked her a question. I immediately liked what I

could see of Erin, but I found Jim overly smooth, overly confident, overly critical, and exceptionally elusive to my psychological "scanner." It seemed to me
that I wasn't seeing the real Jim, that maybe he was hiding something.

When I saw them individually at subsequent sessions, I tried to remedy
the earlier situation. I fed Erin a lot of questions and gave her plenty of
room to talk. She did! I heard all about a marriage that was lived in the
shadow of Jim's big, successful, dominating family—a family that was rich
and well-educated and unusually sure of itself.

With Jim, I tried to get him off of his ice skates. That is, I wanted to keep
him from skating away from me, from smoothly avoiding each of my questions. He was trying to get my help in bringing Erin into line without letting
me see his role in the problem.

Here is what I began to discover from those individual sessions. Erin had
traded her individuality and uniqueness for the status and security of Jim's
money and confidence. She had come from a poor family, and Jim represented a way out. What she didn't know was that while Jim's family had an
abundance of money, they had a serious lack of emotional health. Jim was
confident all right—far too confident. He was too wrapped up in himself,
too well-defended, too unconsciously fragile. He suffered from an emotional
problem called narcissistic personality disturbance. In other words, his needs
completely dominated his life; they overshadowed Erin and their marriage.
There was going to be no good marriage and no good sexual relationship
until Jim addressed his internal fragility.

I must tell you that I was, sadly, unable to help Jim. He had a very hard
time seeing that he was a source of any of the marital problems. It was
obvious to him that Erin was the reason their sex was poor, and that if she
would shape up, the sex and the marriage would improve. He came to me
reluctantly for a short period, kept his distance from me, and tried desperately to help me see that Erin was the real problem. He was fortified within
his emotional defense system. He suffered from a pervasive fear that if he
ever began to soften, he might have to change his life dramatically. He
badly needed to "die to this old self" so that he could build a healthy self-
conception, but he refused to surrender.

There was no way Erin was ever going to trust Jim with her body—let
alone her soul. He was so tied up in his frantic efforts to love himself that
he had little, if any, real love for her. Erin's self-esteem was low, and she
suffered from a mild form of depression. The fact was that she was trapped
in a marriage that called for her to give up her personhood. Fortunately, she
was too healthy to do that.

The bottom line is this: Sometimes sexual difficulties are the consequence of a marital system that has gone bad because one person is emotionally ill. Until this illness is addressed, the sex probably won't get much better. If the sex does get better without any improvement of the real problems, it is not likely to last for long. Sexual health proceeds out of the most sacred inner places for two persons, and it is not likely to be healthy for long unless the partners become genuinely healthy.

Case Study #3: Jane and Mark

Jane and Mark had been married for two years when they came to see me. It was clear they were deeply in love, but they were terribly frustrated with their marriage.

They told me a sad story. Jane came from a divorced home, and from the time she was nine years old she saw her dad only three or four times a year. Even when she was seven or eight years old, Jane knew that her dad was involved with other women. She agonized for her mom, whom Jane saw as an innocent victim. Jane had terribly mixed feelings about her dad. She yearned for him to like her, to want to be with her, but he had married another woman, moved to the east coast, and he had two children with his new wife. He had little time for Jane, and even when they did get together, he seemed preoccupied and ill at ease. Jane suspected that he was involved with other women again.

That deeply painful experience with her father had poisoned Jane's trust of others. And she failed to differentiate between her dad and Mark. If Mark was five minutes late coming home from work, she suspected him. If he was out of the office during the day when she called, she was sure he was with some other woman. Her fears and imagination were running wild. But through all of this, she was ashamed to tell Mark how seriously and frequently she doubted him.

All of this mistrust came out in their sexual relationship. How could she ever give herself to someone she so deeply suspected of violating her? She couldn't! So she went to bed long before he did and often feigned that she was asleep when he came to bed. She had physical illnesses of one kind or another whenever he tried to initiate sex. She had even started sleeping in a different bedroom at times, telling Mark that his snoring kept her awake.

When I discovered what the real issue was, we went to work on Jane's suspicions, her deep and pervasive doubts about the integrity of her husband. This case turned out just the way we hoped and prayed it would. Jane became consciously clear about the extreme differences in the character of her father and her husband. She took control of her unconscious transference. She began to program herself to think twice before she let her suspicions about her father control her perception of her husband. In time, she and Mark developed a trusting relationship, and with some coaching and cheerleading from me, their sex life became thoroughly satisfying to both of them.

Cases I Refer to Other Professionals

Obviously, there are all kinds of reasons for sexual problems. I've told you about three of these, but there are many others. Certain problems I like to refer to people who specialize in sexual therapy. For instance, if a man is impotent, I like to have my colleagues, the Penners, cooperate with his urologist in finding a cure for his impotence. The same is true of premature ejaculation for a man and vaginismus for a woman (a condition in which the vagina remains too tight for penis penetration). Most of these cases can be cured efficiently, but they require a considerable amount of technical expertise.

Nevertheless, the vast majority of sexual problems result from psychological factors, and these issues must be carefully addressed before the sexual relationship is likely to improve. There is no better feeling for a psychotherapist than the elation that comes from a careful management of psychological problems—and a sexual relationship that becomes wonderfully satisfying.

The Critical Contribution of a Spiritual Bond

The best sexual relationship is one that proceeds out of a couple's deep and intimate "soul bonding." Show me a couple for whom feelings and thoughts are shared from the innermost levels, and I'll show you a couple ready to have a triumphant sexual relationship. If their sexual relationship is not triumphant, they probably only need some careful instruction and coaching.

It is spiritual bonding that characterizes the finest marital relationships. Spiritual bonding comes from hard work that is carried out in an atmosphere of deep trust. When spiritual bonding is established, sex is a lot more than the merging of body parts. What really happens is that the souls of two people get woven together. This is even more important than orgasm, but orgasm is likely to happen when the spiritual bond develops. This is when euphoria is experienced!

A Five-Step Plan for a 10 Percent Gain

Marriages in North America would be enormously enhanced if couples could experience a 10 percent gain in the mutual satisfaction level of their sexual relationship. I am totally confident that any couple who reads this book can experience this 10 percent improvement in their sexual relationship within the next six months. The plan is straightforward, but it does require some regular collaboration of both spouses.

1. **You both must be willing to try.** If you can say to each other that you would like to take this challenge together, and that you're willing to work on it over the next six months, you have completed the first of five simple steps. Reminder: As a couple, you are not trying for perfection in the sexual area of your relationship. You may not be trying for anything close to perfection! You're simply trying to improve your sexual relationship by 10 percent over a six-month period, and you're committed to working this five-step plan. Whatever you do, don't put yourself under the stress of unrealistic expectations. Figure out what a 10 percent improvement would be for the two of you, and then get about the job of doing these five things.

2. **Buy a good book on marital sex.** I recommend *Restoring the Pleasure* by Clifford and Joyce Penner.[3] Make an agreement with each other to read a chapter (preferably out loud) three times a week. Read each chapter fully, and take time to discuss any exercises that are recommended. When you finish this, you have completed step two, and you are well on your way to improving your sexual relationship by 10 percent.

3. **If either of you experienced sexual abuse in your childhood, immediately begin processing the trauma.** Select a competent and caring professional in your area—or join a counseling group—to help you experience wholeness as completely and thoroughly as possible.

4. **Husbands, practice taking an affirming and responsive role in the sexual relationship.** Start listening to your wife both emotionally and spiritually. Ask her questions about herself, and then listen, listen, listen. Practice the various suggestions the Penners made earlier: (A) affirm your wife, let her take the lead, and then respond to her; (B) proceed slowly; (C) allow her to guide the process, but follow close behind; (D) be into the sexual process for the pleasure of it, rather than for the result of it.

5. **Learn to talk freely as a couple about your sexual feelings.** Many couples find it awkward and embarrassing to talk about their sexual needs. But

relying on guesswork usually isn't very helpful. Work hard at being completely open about your sexual needs, and work even harder at understanding what the other person's needs are. Encourage each other to take initiative in the sexual process, but make sure that both of you wish to proceed before you get further involved.

If you and your spouse will follow this simple plan for six months, I strongly suspect that your sexual relationship will be a full 10 percent better. If it is, you have done something together of gigantic importance for the future of your marriage. The secret is to keep working at this for six months. Persistence and the right attitude will bring dramatic results.

How much hope is there for the sexual relationship in your marriage? All kinds! If you will follow this five-step program, I am totally confident that your sexual relationship can grow by leaps and bounds. Follow these five steps faithfully for six months, and see if your sexual relationship isn't 10 percent better. If it is, what might another six months of dedicated work mean for the two of you?

Get Connected

Recognize the Role of Children and Friends in Making Your Marriage Triumphant

"Our daughter and son have greatly enhanced our marriage. The unbelievable mystery of human life—a unique blend of us both—creates a profound bond. The times of conflict, though real and painful, have been far less frequent than the times of celebration. The shared values and experiences are bridges of intimacy."

—a man from Minnesota

"We have lots and lots of friends! We cherish friendships with a wide variety of adults and children of all ages. They have supported and enriched us and are definitely a measure of our good fortune."

—a woman from Washington State

The couples in our survey presented two themes with more intensity than all others. The first had to do with commitment and trust. Without these qualities in a marriage, the 100 extremely healthy couples held out little hope for the building of a triumphant relationship.

The other strongly held conviction was woven around children. Over 90 of the 100 couples stressed the vital contribution to their marriages that their children had made. Many of the couples made it clear that friends had played a substantial role, too. But their passion had to do with children, and they could hardly speak positively enough.

Everybody knows that children require backbreaking work from the time they push their little heads out of the birth canal and say hello to this big world. They have to be picked up when they cry, carried everywhere, fed and bathed regularly, worried about, listened to when they fuss, taken to every kind of doctor, taught everything they know, and prayed for without ceasing. What in the world makes them so important to a great marriage?

Children have to be loved unconditionally, trusted to "look both ways," held accountable, praised, shaped, reinforced, encouraged, disciplined, treated with patience and understanding . . . and don't forget, they must be "prayed for without ceasing." How is it that we think of them as crucial to marital fulfillment?

Then there's the matter of economics. Children cost us so much money. You start paying for them from the moment you think you might be pregnant, and you keep paying for them until . . . until you decide to quit paying for them. You pay doctor bills and hospital bills that strap you for every dollar you've saved. You buy clothes and baby furniture and diapers and rattles and bottles and formula. You buy more new clothes every three months, toys of every kind, shoes and more shoes. You pay for lessons they don't even want to take, PTA memberships, more of those doctor bills and antibiotics.

You have to help children crawl right and stand right and walk right. You have to move all your possessions out of their way. You have to bribe them and threaten them and tempt them. You guard them with your life, give them your last ounce of energy . . . and more of that "praying for them without ceasing."

Then they get older and start pretending you're not that important to them anymore. They want you out of their way. They long to be rid of you. But they want some more money, and they want to be picked up at the mall, and they want—are you ready for this?—your car! This kid wants your car, the one you have worked for and saved for and cared for. And he wants it clean! With gas!

So what is it about children that makes over 90 of our 100 extremely successful couples name them as crucial to the happiness of their marriage?

"Half My Genes and Half Yours"

After all these years of listening to people talk about their children, I've become convinced that most of their passion revolves around the mystery represented by the blending of both spouses' physical, emotional, and intellectual qualities. It's the magical combination of "half my genes and half yours." There is something mind-boggling about the idea that the love of my life and I can somehow merge our uniqueness—our very beings—in a little person who will live with us and be around us for the rest of our lives. And this little being will be an incredible blend of you and me. We can have a little us.

I remember the birth of our first child like it was yesterday. Lorrie was born after we had been at the hospital for only 40 minutes, so she was wide awake, pink and white, and more beautiful than anything I had ever seen in my life. I watched her being given her first "shower," and then I went down to see Marylyn as they were bringing her back from the delivery room. Still groggy, she looked up at me and asked if everything was all right.

I interrupted her to say, "We have the most magnificent little girl I have ever seen!"

Even in her grogginess, Marylyn squealed with delight. I hugged her, and we cried together. We both recall this moment as the most inspirational experience of our entire marriage. It was our first taste of "half my genes and half yours." When you encounter the mystery of human life from such an up-close vantage point, you cannot fail to sense the powerful presence of God.

Because of the way biology works, there is no other means by which two lovers can merge and blend so profoundly as they do in their children. If merging and blending are at the heart of the love experience, then children make love happen between two people at levels that are otherwise impossible. Every cell of this child is made up of us. Every propensity is the result of our combined essence. There is something about knowing all this that sends romantic shivers down our spines.

The unity and oneness of a couple is never so obvious as when we see our children. Children represent, both biologically and emotionally, the fusion of our beings. It is this fusion that contributes so significantly to the sacredness of marriage. It is clear evidence that God has taken the essence of you and me and made us "one flesh."

"Look What Great Kids We Have Made Together"

Several of our surveyed couples discussed their bursting pride for the wonderful children they have. They discussed the significance to their marriage that they had together participated in the formation of such beautiful young lives. And they should be proud! At the risk of sounding naively simplistic, let me say that after 30 years of working with couples and families, I am convinced of the strong correlation between the emotional atmosphere created by the parents in the home and the emotional health of their children. The factors that contribute to children turning out well are not confusing, nor do they primarily involve luck and chance. If parents end up with great children, they should be delighted with themselves, for they have obviously done many things right.

I hasten to add, however, that parents whose children are troubled should not immediately leap from the nearest cliff. The factors that relate to the development of pain-filled children often relate far less to the role of parents than do the factors that lead to extremely healthy children. In other words, parents can often take credit for rearing good kids, but the parents of troubled kids shouldn't always take the blame. You may wonder if I can prove this point, and I believe I can.

I readily admit that when children develop in an unhealthy way, their parents often contribute to their development. Show me a family in which parents fight a lot, are overly involved in their individual lives, or model for their children the broken lives which they had modeled for them by their parents, and I will show you children whose pain is directly related to the contributions of their parents.

But I can immediately think of four factors (and there are probably more), which have little to do with the input of parents, that contribute to the unfortunate development of kids. If, for instance, a child suffers from a learning disability and acquires a negative self-conception, the parents are not responsible for this. The same is true if the child is physically or sexually abused at an early age by someone outside the family, someone totally beyond the control of the parents. I think also about children who become dominated by peers who are mean and somehow steal influence from the parents. And I think about children who are born with fewer natural gifts and are "sitting ducks" for the scorn and harshness of their peers. All of these scenarios may contribute to the troubles of a young person—and parents cannot be blamed for them.

This is not a book about the validation or invalidation of parents on the basis of how their children turn out. It is a book about what contributes to a triumphant marriage. What I'm telling you is that of the 100 marriages recommended to me by people around North America, the vast majority cited "children" as vital to the excellence of their marriages. And a careful analysis of this dramatic result reveals that parents often experience a deep sense of oneness with each other when they observe their children, and when they end up saying something like "We really did a great job together."

When Children Drain Energy From a Marriage

One woman in our study has four little boys who are five years of age and under. She said: "Our children have enhanced our relationship incredibly, but they have also put physical and emotional demands on my husband and me that make it tough to have energy for each other."

Another woman with four older children said: "What a joy and a blessing they all are, but if we didn't have kids, life would undoubtedly be easier and the quality of our relationship would be different. I believe our relationship is good for the time my husband and I are able to spend together, but we both look forward to when it will be just the two of us again."

We can't deny that rearing children requires an enormous amount of energy, and there is seldom enough energy to supply all the family needs. The marriage often gets slighted. Sometimes the needs and demands of the children seem urgent, so the needs of the marriage (which may be seen as important but not urgent) are put on hold. Depending on the health of the marriage, this "waiting" period may be managed fairly easily for a while. But many relationships are badly wounded by the neglect that occurs when children take priority over the marriage.

Some people look back on their neglected marriages with regret. One woman said: "I think I failed in this area. When the kids were growing up, I put them ahead of Bob many times, and I met their needs more than his. I was always there for them, and Bob took a back seat. He may not say it, but I could have done a better job here."

The majority of parents say that children are most demanding—and thus the marriage can suffer the most—during two stages: preschool and adolescence. Children require an unusual amount of energy between the time of their birth and the time they enter kindergarten. After that the years go fairly smoothly, until the children reach adolescence (usually 13 to 18 years of age). During these periods, parents often feel "used up" and relatively unavailable for each other. Sometimes, husbands and wives find it extremely difficult to spend time alone together during these high-demand years. They may become distant from one another, feel unloved and unimportant, and sense that all the romance has vanished from their relationship.

I have frequently counseled couples to be aware of those critical periods. I encourage them to find a solution before resentment sets in. Resentment is a virus; when it gets a foothold in a marriage, it can multiply rapidly. Then the problems build on each other. The husband feels unimportant to his wife, so he spends more time at work or playing golf. She experiences his absence as rejection, worries about what it means, and unconsciously defends against the threat of it by investing even more of herself in the children. This process can build such momentum of its own that marital deterioration suddenly becomes frighteningly difficult to stop.

None of this destructive process is necessary. There are two main antidotes that will keep any marriage free of the negative effects of children:

Antidote #1: Both Partners Need to Be Enthusiastic About the Child-Rearing Process

Obviously, the matter of parenting needs to be a subject that receives vital attention prior to a couple's decision to marry. If one partner is enthusiastic about having children and the other wants no part of it, how can they ever achieve a great relationship? If one partner is ambivalent about children and the other eagerly anticipates becoming a parent, they had better take plenty of time before moving forward—let that ambivalent partner figure out what he or she really thinks about parenting.

The fact is that rearing children is enormously difficult. Even though some single parents do a good job, most of them will tell you how totally exhausting the task really is. Child rearing requires the best effort of both a mom and a dad, and when one of them isn't interested or excited or energized, the whole endeavor suffers tremendously.

I encourage parents to recognize what a vital part child rearing can play in their lives together. When they take it on as partners, when they see what a sacred privilege it is, when they come to recognize that rearing great kids is a goal worth pursuing, they are headed toward something wonderful. Children contribute greatly to a triumphant marriage if a man and woman are equal partners in the task, if they both deeply love their offspring, and if they recognize that sometimes the energy required to meet the demands will take everything they've got.

This is the big picture that a husband and a wife need to be clear about all along the child-rearing path. If they are, they will be able to rise to the challenge—and thoroughly enjoy the process. And when they stand back to marvel at their kids, they will secretly be saying to each other: "Oh my, hasn't this been wonderful? How very much I love you when I look at these children of ours. This partnership of ours is such a strong and healthy one."

Antidote #2: There Must Be Time for Romance All Along the Way

Show me a man and a woman who have children, and I will show you a man and a woman who need more than ever to nurture their relationship and make sure it thrives and grows.

There is something about romance that is intensely personal. It all gets started when two people look at each other and feel something powerful happening inside themselves. They sit down with each other and begin to share their thoughts and feelings. They talk about their dreams and goals, their values and beliefs, their hopes and fears. These two lovers will never outgrow their need to look at one another, share with each other from the most central part of themselves, and be assured that the other person cherishes them and respects them.

There are few, if any, happily married persons I know who can get what they need from one another without engaging in this very personal, very direct process. They simply cannot expect the other person to be fed and nurtured on the basis of a "reflected" message. Sometimes, men who spend tremendous amounts of energy in their careers want their wives to feel their love on the basis of "how hard I am working for both of us." It doesn't work like this! And sometimes, women who give passionately to their children want their husbands to "see how much I obviously love you because of how much I am giving to our kids." It doesn't work like this, either!

Romance requires personal time. There is never a time when two people can keep their love growing and prospering without plenty of energy spent relating to each other individually and intimately.

Whatever it is that demands our energy, it becomes a threat to our romance. It really doesn't matter if this demand involves our work, kids, aged parents, church, health, or possessions. Whatever requires so much energy that we reduce our energy for romance, this becomes a marital threat for us. This is why I encourage people who have children—especially small children or adolescents—to schedule time for their romance, to make time for it at least once a week. This time investment will pay incredible dividends if it is done well.

The Interdependence of Marital Health and Thriving Children

When I read all 200 surveys of spouses in great marriages, I wondered whether "successful children" create triumphant marriages or whether triumphant marriages tend to spawn successful children.

There is no question that when children are healthy—when they do well in school, are well adjusted to their peer group, and feel good about their family life—it is far easier for parents to flourish in their marriage. Children who develop in a happy and healthy way are incredibly validating to their parents.

Similarly, when children are physically ill, do poorly in school, have few friends, suffer from learning disabilities, and don't enjoy family life very much, their parents can easily doubt themselves—and their marriage may well suffer.

The reality is that a great marriage provides optimal conditions for a child to do well. And a child's success often contributes to the health of a marriage. My many years of clinical work have confirmed to me that the best way to build great families is to build great marriages. I am aware of how vitally children can contribute to a marriage, but an unhealthy marriage seldom gets healthy on the basis of the success of the children. Of course, children are seldom emotionally healthy or happy when their parents are not well loved by each other.

The secret of a well-connected family system is almost always a function of a carefully nurtured love relationship between the two parents. Keeping this love relationship in the best emotional shape is the fundamental challenge for every man and woman who ventures into the family-building business.

Should Parents Stay Together Just for Their Children?

Parents should stay together because they promised to—not for their children! If a marital relationship has become horribly painful and poisonous, are children better off if parents leave one another, or if they stay together?

Countless social analysts in the 1970s and 1980s argued that every married person should determine for himself or herself the path that would provide the greatest amount of personal satisfaction and growth. If this meant divorce, and even if this divorce might shatter their children and/or spouse, these individuals were encouraged to proceed with divorce. The thinking was: Do whatever you need to in order to be happy—even if your loved ones are trampled in the process. This era of individualism has been dramatically reversed in recent years. This reversal has been spurred by research that reveals how disastrous divorce is for children.

For instance, Professor Judith Wallerstein of the University of California undertook in 1970 a longitudinal project designed to study the development of children from broken homes.[1] She gathered a sample of 131 children, all of whose parents were in the process of divorce. When she interviewed these children 18 months after the breakup, she concluded that there was not a single emotionally healthy child in the group—and not a single child for whom their parents' divorce was not the major event of their life. Professor Wallerstein followed these children through the years, and in 1995 she declared that one-half of all the children are still suffering from emotional disturbances directly traceable to their parents' divorces.

Further, Professor Sara McClanahan at Princeton University completed a tightly controlled study of the effects of divorce on children. She concluded that girls whose parents had divorced were significantly more likely than their peers to drop out of high school and to become teen mothers.

Throughout North America, there is a strong effort to encourage parents to remain married because of the disastrous consequences of divorce on children. But I have deep concern about any reasoning that promotes continuing marriages without strong efforts to strengthen marriages. I believe passionately in the continuation of all marriages, but the argument that marriage should be maintained "for the children" is a very dangerous one.

It contributes to a superficial understanding of the sanctity of marriage. The idea that a marriage should be held together for anything external—even something as critical and wonderful as children—draws attention away from the miraculous nature of marriage itself. Marriage involves a covenant between a man and a woman to love, honor, and cherish each other for a lifetime. It is on the basis of this covenant that marriage is held to be eternal. To distract attention from this central covenant is what creates concern for me.

My own bias is that marriage is fundamentally a spiritual matter. When a man and woman pledge their undying love to each other, they are joined together by God. This is the miracle of marriage. This is also the reason that divorce is so hurtful to the human soul—and to the larger community as well. Moreover, I strongly believe that every couple can keep their promises; they can make their relationship better and better over time if they decide to work at it. They may not choose to work this hard, but they can be successful.

Yes, parents should stay together. By staying together they will create dramatically better chances for their children to have full, happy lives. But if they stay together only for their kids, if they just "stay together" and do almost nothing to make their relationship more loving, more satisfying for both of them, no real resolution has been reached. Their kids deserve more than their just "staying together." They deserve their parents' best efforts to make their relationship really work.

Seven Principles for Highly Effective Parenting

Some couples are far more effective in their parenting than other couples are. Whether they know it or not, they utilize certain principles that result in healthy development for their child and for their relationship with their child. Consequently, these parents often experience their children as reinforcers of their marriages.

I have watched thousands of parents with their children. I have often had an opportunity to see how these relationships turned out, and I've gained a strong sense of what works and what doesn't work. Here is my list of seven parenting principles for the development of great kids.

Principle #1: Your Child Is a Separate Being

Parents who are successful tell me that no other principle is as important as this one! As a parent, you are a "trustee." You do not own your children. You have them for only a short while, and then they will leave you.

This means, of course, that you should not try to make them into a carbon copy of yourself. It is all right to give them your name if you choose, but it is not all right to expect that they will be just like you. They may become remarkably different from you. They have a separate identity, they are created with a different biochemical system from any person on earth, they have unique personalities, and they will ultimately determine their own destiny. They are separate beings!

Principle #2: You Have Been Entrusted with the Sacred Task of Helping Your Children Become Everything They Are Capable of Becoming

A fundamental part of your parenting task is to help your child discover his or her talents, strengths, interests, gifts, and natural abilities. This discovery often requires listening on the part of parents. Great parents listen to gain information about their child's essential likes and dislikes, interests, needs, hurts, and hopes. This process also takes keen observation, as you watch and determine where your child's natural talents lie.

Once identified, these talents must be nurtured and cultivated. You must give your child the opportunity to grow and expand. It is your job to help your child reach his or her full potential.

When parents handle this task conscientiously, their child's eventual identity will once more reflect the awesome creativity of the Creator. And the relationship that will develop between these parents and this little child will be rich and satisfying. When the task of parenting is done right, there is nothing like it in the world. One of its finest by-products is that it makes two parents grow together as they never have before.

Principle #3: Vital to Your Child's Development Will Be a Consistent Experience of Being Loved Unconditionally

Absolutely nothing is more important to psychological development than a child's basic sense that his or her worth is never in jeopardy, that he is loved simply because of who he is—not on the basis of any conditional factors. Love isn't given and taken away because of behavior, performance, intellect, appearance, academic achievement, or any other component. Love is just given—no questions asked, nothing demanded in return. It is this experience that will allow him to develop to the full extent of his capacity.

So why don't some parents love their children unconditionally? I believe parents are able to love their child unconditionally to the degree to which they have experienced unconditional love themselves. I would be less than candid if I did not tell you how frustrated I get at my own inability to love unconditionally—whether in relation to my wife, children, grandchildren, clients, friends, sisters, or even strangers. It is hard to love people this way!

I have found that I can love this way only when I keep myself strong in my own Christian faith. My parents instilled within me a deep belief that I have been created by a God who loves me to my depths, who could love me no more deeply if I were perfect and no less strongly if I were totally imperfect. The minister of the church I attended when I was young, Harry Robert Fox Jr., and the president of the seminary I attended, John A. MacKay, directed me to the greatest book of the New Testament (at least as I now see it), the letter of the Apostle Paul to the church at Rome. It was here that I discovered a message about the love of Jesus that persists in the face of every kind of force that would deflect it. When I stay in touch with this dynamic, my ability to love unconditionally the people around me becomes greater.

It is this kind of love that children need to experience in relation to their parents. Parents who can share it with their children are likely to have healthy children indeed.

Principle #4: Every Child Needs Carefully Determined and Consistently Maintained Limits

It is essential that parents place limits on their children's behavior. These limits give their children a sense of security, and they protect both the parents and others from out-of-control children.

The determination of these limits is clearly of great importance. If they are set too narrowly, or unrealistically, the child will be filled with frustration and resentment. The result will likely be an angry and hostile child. But the limits can also be set too broadly. This results in excessive permissiveness that is not at all good for the child, for the parents, or for others who must endure the child's behavior.

I recommend that parents spend generous amounts of time in the determination of limits for their children, seek the best advice they can, and work hard to agree on what these limits should be. Then I encourage parents to be highly consistent in maintaining these limits.

Principle #5: Parents Must Decide How to Discipline Their Children in the Most Effective Way

Discipline is absolutely vital to the formation of great kids—and the formation of great parent-child relationships. But the exact details of discipline that parents should adopt are something only they can determine.

I try to make a strong point in my work with parents, a point I made in the earlier chapter on conflict resolution. It comes from the work of B. F. Skinner, the renowned psychologist from Harvard University. His research makes abundantly clear that a child—or anyone else—learns significantly more from being praised for what they do right than from being punished for what they do wrong. The crucial point is that parents need to praise and penalize their child on the basis of carefully determined principles that they apply in a highly consistent way.

Principle #6: A Child Should Be Helped to Dream a Great Dream for His or Her Life

Parents are in a prime position to help their children develop a dream for their lives. Just as parents need a great dream for their marriage, so do children need a life dream. This dream can be modified all along the way, but any dream will stimulate their brains and mobilize their action centers.

Moreover, there is nothing two parents can do for their marriage that will inspire them more than helping their children develop goals—goals that will set them free to stretch and grow as they actualize their potential. Show me a young person with a wonderful dream, and I will show you some active and satisfied parents in the background.

Principle #7: Assisting a Child to Develop Character and Adopt Values Is Crucial

I know of nothing that is quite so gratifying for parents as recognizing that their child has developed attributes of character that will strengthen him for a lifetime. Likewise, when a child identifies values in which he passionately believes and for which he is willing to give his all, both parents and child can be deeply thankful and proud.

Of course, one of the strongest evidences of sterling character is the way the child treats others in the family, including younger siblings and older relatives. Sensitivity in these areas is a sign of deep security, thoughtful reflection, and good judgment.

The Role of Children in a Triumphant Marriage

I have seldom seen a triumphant marriage in which children played no role. Moreover, I have never seen a great marriage in which there was an antagonistic or distant relationship between parents and their children. When there is love between a husband and wife, and where there is strong respect for the children born out of that love, the result is sure to be a family that can relate to one another in deeply meaningful ways. When this kind of connectedness happens within a secure atmosphere, the many shades of love that result almost always make for an overwhelmingly beautiful human fabric. We call this fabric a family.

It is a prize that is unattainable if the husband and wife are not blended by their love and their relational competence. But when there is a dad who loves a mom with a durable, undying love, and when a mom loves a dad with a soft, pure, never-ending affection, the children are sure to benefit greatly.

A triumphant marriage is the context in which any baby would like to find himself or herself. These children will grow up to be emotionally, physically, mentally, spiritually, and socially strong—and they will make any marriage even more triumphant.

Pursue Spirituality

Partners in Great Marriages Find Significance in Their Spiritual Lives

"God saved our marriage. When we rededicated our lives to the Lord, we had divorce papers ready to be signed. We decided to give it one last chance, and since we had tried everything else, we figured we'd give God a chance. What He did for us was a miracle."

—a 50-year-old New York State woman, married 34 years

"Our marital satisfaction can be plotted on a graph that would parallel our spiritual breakthroughs. When I came to know God, I stopped taking false blame and became a free person. Carol could begin to relax—and trust and respect me in new ways. A personal, intimate spiritual encounter with God made all the difference in me and our marriage."

—a man from Minnesota

When two lovers are both spiritually sensitive, I suspect their marriage is destined to be triumphant. What an incredible difference it makes to both of them to know that they are fellow travelers on a spiritual journey.

There is a dramatic resurgence of spirituality all over North America. The November 28, 1994, issue of *Newsweek* focused on this heightened interest in spiritual things:

> From Wall Streeters to artists, from Andre Agassi to David Mamet, millions of Americans are embarking on a search for the sacred in their lives. Whether out of dissatisfaction with the material world or worried about the coming millennium, they are seeking to put spirituality back in their lives. For careerist baby boomers, it's even OK to use the S words—soul, sacred, spiritual, sin.

The 100 couples in our sample consistently cited some form of spirituality as crucial to the development of their extremely healthy marriages. They pointed out what has been recognized for a long time—that when a couple gets spiritually healthy, they automatically move toward marital harmony and oneness. There is something miraculously bonding for two lovers when they experience significant overlap in the spiritual realm.

I find that writing about spiritual matters seems fraught with danger. Maybe that's because of the tendency of some people to impose their spiritual understandings on others and to assume that everyone should live out these intricate and intimate areas exactly as they do. Or maybe any discussion of "spiritual strength" sounds like the speaker is bragging—like he's saying, "God is on my side" or "I've got the market cornered on this particular teaching." We simply want to run when someone boasts about his "spiritual victories."

Yet as a clinician who has worked with couples for three decades, I know that you can't talk about a triumphant marriage without including the spiritual dimension. And the couples I surveyed confirmed this. When all these inventories came rolling in, I knew for sure that one of the key secrets of a great marriage is the ability of a couple to "plumb their spiritual depths."

A Story That Greatly Affected My Marriage

I am especially uneasy about discussing my own spiritual experience. I feel confident that if you and I could be together face-to-face, you would understand the combination of passion and reserve I feel in this area. You would come to know my sense of awe in relation to the spiritual realm, but you would also recognize my reluctance to impose my experience on you.

With all of this in mind, I want to tell you a story that involves me, my wife, and our oldest daughter, Lorrie, and her husband, Greg.

Greg and Lorrie's oldest son, Matt, was four years old, and Joe, son number two, was one and a half when Lorrie told us she was pregnant a third time. Marylyn and I were delighted, but somewhat concerned as well—concerned because Lorrie's blood pressure had escalated so rapidly toward the end of her delivery of Joe. Nevertheless, we were ready for the next nine months, and we eagerly anticipated the addition of another grandchild.

Early in the pregnancy, Lorrie's doctor did a sonogram and discovered two babies in the womb. Both appeared to be boys. But the doctor couldn't see the outline of a "sac" for each child, and what later became obvious was that both boys were in the same sac (the technical term for this is monoamniotic). Statistically, about 50 percent of these cases have "somewhat negative" to "extremely negative" outcomes. That's because the babies circle each other so often in the one sac that they get their umbilical cords wrapped into knots. These knots can cut off some or all of the nutrients needed to help the babies develop.

As Lorrie's pregnancy continued, we all grew more and more aware of the dangers. Dr. Macer, her obstetrician, was well-known for his management of difficult pregnancies, but even so, the odds were frightening. At 27 weeks, Lorrie entered the hospital. Full term is 40 weeks, and Dr. Macer was hoping she could keep the babies in the womb for at least 34 weeks. The heart rates of both babies were monitored around the clock. If either boy's heart rate dropped rapidly or stayed low for several minutes, the doctor planned to perform a ceasarean section immediately. The problem, of course, is that the more premature a baby is when born, the less likely its chance of survival.

Our whole community of friends and family prayed for Lorrie. Our close friend Nell Privett organized a network of prayer partners. Every day Lorrie held those babies was a victory; each day made their survival that much more possible.

Every few days, the heart rate of one of the babies would decelerate, and great concern would fill all of us. One night after 29 weeks, Greg called us in the middle of the night from the hospital to report the most serious crisis of the pregnancy. It looked for sure like they were going to have to do a C-section.

I'll never forget what happened to us that night. We hung up the phone, and Marylyn took my hand and said, "Let's pray." To the best of our ability, we poured out our hearts to God, asking Him to protect those two little babies who were trying so hard to make it. We prayed for Lorrie, who was giving everything she had to help them. Marylyn and I held on to one another as tightly as we could, and we put into words our deepest feelings.

Needless to say, we were deeply thankful a few hours later when Greg called to say that the heart rates had returned to normal and that the danger, at least for the time being, had subsided. Through more ups and downs, Lorrie held on until week 34. The time came for them to introduce those boys to the world. They would perform a C-section that day.

Marylyn and I sought the prayers of our friends, and Joe Forgatch, Greg's father, led a strong prayer in Lorrie's room before Dr. Macer came to take her for delivery. Though her blood pressure climbed to perilous heights, Lorrie gave birth to two little boys—healthy, pink, identical, and full of life. William Thomas and Warren Gregory owe their lives in more than a usual way to the God who enabled their mom to lie in that hospital bed for 50 days so they could "ripen."

Moments after their birth, Dr. Macer brought pictures to those of us outside the delivery room. Because this was such an unusual case, he was eager to study all of the details. One of those pictures showed that the boys' umbilical cords were tangled so much that in one place, there were 11 knots. I asked Dr. Macer how those knots kept from being pulled tight and cutting off the nutrients.

"That's what we don't know," he said.

Inside my head at that moment flashed the image of all those friends who had prayed so faithfully—and of the night when Marylyn and I held each other and poured out our hearts to God.

Why Does Shared Spirituality Enhance Marriage So Much?

When two people cling to each other in a crisis and pour out their feelings to a God they both trust and love, there is a merging and blending that weaves them together at their deepest levels. As a matter of fact, I'm convinced that spirituality is especially beneficial for a couple when it involves the deeper ranges of their thinking and feeling—the parts of their life-processing that are far below the superficial levels on which they sometimes operate.

These deeper levels that get drawn into the spiritual search are especially crucial because they often involve those life situations in which we feel unusually desperate, deeply inadequate, intensely in need of help from someone with power and understanding well beyond our own. These are levels we seldom access when we are not in crisis. But our unconscious minds frequently wrestle with these profound aspects of our existence. These are the weighty matters of the human condition that none of us can fully avoid.

That's why a married couple profits so much when they can spiritually process life together. When Marylyn and I held on to each other in the middle of the night, we spoke together to God about matters with which we were passionately concerned. We were forced to put into words what were for us almost inexpressible hopes and feelings. Thereby Marylyn became more intimately acquainted with a part of me that is central to my being. The same was true for me. In that moment, we touched each other at our depths, and we became welded together far more significantly.

What Is the Role of Passion in All of This?

If passion involves extremely strong feelings, there is no question that the prayers Marylyn and I said that night were passionate. In another realm, our sexual communication is passionate, too, but not passionate like those prayers. Interestingly, sexuality and spirituality, I believe, overlap to a surprising degree. They both involve intimate parts of our beings. We must be healthy and secure in these parts of ourselves if we are to have a triumphant marriage. Both sexuality and spirituality participate in that level of our inner selves where our deepest feelings exist.

Why is it so important for a marriage that people be in harmony when it comes to extremely strong feelings? That's where life really matters! That's where we desperately want to share life with the person we love and respect the most.

Think for a moment about how thoroughly our spiritual selves get involved with passion. When we are spiritual, we tend to be involved with life-and-death issues. We turn more directly to God when it comes to situations over which we have little or no control—but about which we care deeply. We speak to God when our own efforts and attempts at effectiveness have run their course. And this is exactly why virtually everything that is spiritually shared in a marriage involves the intimate. It is intimacy taken to the deepest level, intimacy that is richer and purer than any other form of intimacy we know.

This is the reason any couple who develops their capacity to share their spiritual quests is destined to have a triumphant marriage. The two lovers overcome the greatest of all marital enemies—emotional distance. They become joined and merged and blended and interwoven right where they are most wonderfully made—where the spiritual quest happens within them.

When Partners Take Different Spiritual Paths

For better or worse, there are scores of spiritual paths people often take to deal with the profound questions I mentioned above. In a stimulating speech given by Norman Lear, the popular television producer, at the National Press Club in December of 1993, many of the "spiritual paths" people take were identified and described. Lear believes that throughout North America, there is a "buzzing, disconnected eruption of spiritual reaction to our times." He believes that this quest for spiritual significance is the most powerful theme of our culture.

In the middle of all this spiritual searching, we may wonder what happens when marriage partners proceed down two very different paths. I believe that if they do, one of two outcomes is likely. Either they will each need to keep their spiritual pursuit quiet and private, or they will find themselves frequently in conflict.

It is precisely at the point where the spiritual quest is most passionate and most intimate that two people need to be most in harmony. If one person, for instance, is pursuing a course that leaves out God completely and the other person prays to God regularly and seeks after His guidance, how can this couple be anything other than distant from each other?

That night that our grandsons were flirting with tragedy, Marylyn and I called on all of our spiritual harmony. When she took my hand and said "Let's pray," we as a couple were joined in an intense and special way. Marylyn and I both knew that the God to Whom we were praying was our God. In our particular case, this God of ours is "the father of our Lord Jesus Christ." In other words, we identify our God on the basis of His having revealed Himself fully in Jesus. We think of our God as deeply caring about all persons, but especially about children. We both believe that God can be accessed through a spiritual process we label prayer. Marylyn and I are convinced that the way to pray is to merge our deepest feelings with our strongest faith in God. When we "poured out our hearts" about Lorrie and the boys, we moved in unison, we spoke in harmony, and we thought in concert with one another.

As I describe our similarities, I am struck by the extent of them. Some of these similarities we possessed when we were married 39 years ago, some of them we have negotiated over time, and some of them we experienced that very night in the depths of our love for Lorrie and her boys. But the vital point is that the similarities themselves, in this deepest of all spiritual arenas, is what left both Marylyn and me feeling merged and blended, bonded and woven. Undoubtedly, the spiritual quest is significantly more effective when two lovers agree on the path to take. What's more, I am confident that the spiritual dimension contributes to a triumphant marriage to the degree that this spiritual agreement exists.

The Essence of Spiritual Pursuits

In a poll of 756 adults conducted by *Newsweek* magazine in November of 1994, 60 percent of those questioned said they think "a person needs to believe in God in order to experience the sacred." Fifty percent of the respondents reported that they "feel a deep sense of the sacred all or most of the time in church or at worship services." Outside of church, 45 percent sense the sacred during meditation, 68 percent at the birth of a child, and 26 percent during sex.

Having been raised on biblical, Judeo-Christian teachings, God has always been at the center of my spiritual quest. But it was long after I became a psychologist that I began to understand more deeply and believe more passionately in God. My passion was ignited when I began to study more fully the writings of the New Testament. I discovered there a description of God—in the life and teachings of Jesus—that I find irresistibly attractive.

Most of the people I see in my clinical practice are on a spiritual quest. (The statistics above make it clear that "most Americans" are on this journey. In fact, the *Newsweek* poll found that 58 percent "feel the need to experience spiritual growth.") I have noted that when this quest is centered on a God who is love and the source of love, the quest almost always leads to emotional and relational wholeness. But when their quest is less organized and less focused, when it does not center on this loving God, the quest almost always stagnates well before the person has arrived at the goal of emotional health. The same factors are involved in spiritually and emotionally healthy marriages.

Can Spiritual Searching Lead to Marital Deterioration?

The specter of religious fanaticism that is hate-filled and judgmental, that is devoid of kindness and gentleness, is an ugly one. I have never seen even a decent marriage in which one or both persons could fall under this label.

As a matter of fact, I can't help but think that any spiritual quest that does not lead to positive emotional health has gone down the wrong path. In one of the greatest chapters in the New Testament—chapter 5 of his letter to the church in Galatia—the apostle Paul indicates that a healthy spiritual search will result in a person's being filled by the Holy Spirit. When this happens, Paul says, they will be full of "love, joy, peace, patience, kindness, goodness, faithfulness, gentleness and self-control" (Galatians 5:22-23). This list is repeated in several other places, and it is almost identical from place to place.

Any marriage in which both persons have these attributes is destined to be triumphant. Think how easy it would be to live with a person who demonstrates these qualities.

Paul recognizes, however, that there is what he calls "warfare" in the spiritual realm. One force he interprets as "our natural desires"; the other force is the Holy Spirit. He says that "these two forces within us are constantly fighting each other to win control over us, and our wishes are never free from their pressures" (Galatians 5:17). When a person is ruled by "their natural desires," Paul indicates that all kinds of problems will be caused that could create chaos in marriage: "hatred and fighting, jealousy and anger, constant effort to get the best for yourself, complaints and criticisms, the feeling that everyone else is wrong except those in your own little group" (verse 20). Think how these attitudes and actions could wipe out a marriage!

Thus, for Paul, a battle is involved in the spiritual arena, and the clear winner will be the person for whom the Holy Spirit takes control. It is this phenomenon that leads to a great life and a great marriage.

The Excitement of Looking Beyond Yourself

Brett and Tiffany came to me after 10 years of marriage. They weren't fighting with each other that much; they didn't have enough energy for that. Their problem was that they were painfully bored with their life together.

I asked them to tell me about a typical week. Tiffany started with Monday morning: "Brett leaves for work at 7:15," she said in a depressed-sounding voice. "I get the three kids off to school. Brett works all day, the three kids are in school all day, and I clean the house and wash the clothes."

There was a pause—a long pause—and I observed them and waited for one of them to continue. Now they had me bored! I thought it might be the right time for a good joke or some aerobics, but then again, I wondered if we should all just take a nap.

"Is that the extent of it?" I asked with little life in my voice.

"Well," Tiffany said, "the kids come home at 3:35, and Brett gets home at 5:00, unless one of the kids has a game, and then we eat. . . ."

It doesn't take any brilliance to note that the one thing she said that had a shred of interest was "unless one of the kids has a game."

"Oh," I said, sitting forward in my chair to get me going, "tell me about the games."

"All three of the kids are on soccer teams, baseball teams, and basketball teams, and we go to all their games," Brett interjected.

"You go to all their games?" I asked incredulously.

"Yes," Tiffany said, "the kids wouldn't be happy if we missed any of their games. We're always there."

I was beginning to see why their relationship had gone dead. They lived the same humdrum routine week after week, month after month. I won't bore you with the rest of this story! Suffice it to say, I kept questioning, and I kept getting the same dull, monotonous answers that filled me with the listlessness of their lives.

But let me get right to the point. So many marriages are dead because they are constricted. The environment in which the marriages are lived is pitifully small. "We get up, we practice our routine, we come home, we eat, we do our chores, we go to bed, we sleep."

How do you enlarge the environment in which your marriage exists? How about starting with the spiritual! Move out of your narrowly focused world and aim your sights toward the larger world—and the world beyond the larger world.

Suppose Tiffany and Brett were to get involved with an active, enthusiastic church. How might that contribute to the scope of their lives and the energy of their daily existence?

First, they would be drawn into a lively dialogue about the most crucial issues involved in living. They would be challenged to think about why they are on the earth at all, whether anyone is in charge, and if so, whether this sovereign being is knowable. They would be swept up in a new way of processing their experience, relating to the infinite, dealing with each other and every person on the face of the earth. They would be singing and praying and laughing and thinking and feeling more deeply than before. They would be caring more passionately. They would come alive! And as they came alive individually, their marriage would come alive!

They wouldn't have time to sit through game after game after game every week—trying to generate some excitement by over-identifying with their kids or fighting with the adults who were coaching them. They would be too busy with stimulating and useful projects of their own. Not too busy to be with their kids or to take an interest in their kids' feelings about their games or even how the games turned out—but too busy to sit there being bored to death.

Ideally, their conversations at dinner with each other would be filled with current events and with concern for the world. Maybe they would think together about a Bible passage like the one in 1 John 4:7-8—

> Dear friends, let us practice loving each other, for love comes from God and those who are loving and kind show that they are the children of God, and that they are getting to know him better. But if a person isn't loving and kind, it shows that he doesn't know God—for God is love.

Show me a family that talks around the dinner table about the importance of caring about other people in the world, and I'll show you a family that is alive and healthy.

Spirituality is crucial for any couple, and any couple's family. If spiritual concerns are ignored, the material world becomes very confining. The size of the universe drastically shrinks. But when a couple gets in touch with the all-encompassing issues, with the questions that are as big as creation itself, they will have minds and hearts that are eager for tomorrow morning to come.

So are you wondering what happened to Brett and Tiffany? They did, in fact, get involved in a healthy, caring, vital church like the one I described. You know why? Brett's boss invited them there as his guests because he saw how dead Brett's life was and how seriously his work was being affected. By getting involved in something exciting and challenging, and by turning their focus to the world beyond their own, Brett and Tiffany's marriage took on new vigor. They still had some issues to work through, of course, but their major source of trouble—boredom—all but disappeared.

The Difference Between Thinking and Experiencing

Many struggles can arise when a couple dedicates themselves to pursuing spiritual meaning. One of the most constant has to do with the struggle between the cognitive and the affective—between thinking and feeling. As a matter of fact, I frequently note that couples who spend too much time thinking together often lack emotional vitality in their marriage. On the other hand, people who are too deeply into feeling and experiencing suffer from an absence of cognitive structure for their lives—a structure that provides organization and tends to hold life together when things get temporarily out of control.

When I find couples who can be spiritual together—who worship, study, sing, pray, cry, laugh, and talk together—I know they have a great chance of making something special between them. It is this wonderful combination of experiencing and thinking that makes their existence so balanced, so spontaneously ordered, so enjoyable.

So how do you develop this kind of balance in a marriage? First, you recognize it as a goal. Then you think and feel your way to the goal. You pursue writings, teachings, art, music, movies, and plays that help you develop one part or another of this goal. And you watch to make sure that you don't drift too far in one of these directions. In your searching, you seek a healthy balance between thinking and feeling.

Can You Be Spiritually Healthy But Emotionally Unhealthy?

I've concluded that it's not possible to be spiritually healthy and emotionally unhealthy—except for short interludes of time. Think again about how the New Testament apostles Paul and John suggest that we determine whether a person is "in a right relationship with God" or "is filled with the Holy Spirit."

Paul lists the "fruit of the Spirit": love, joy, peace, patience, kindness, goodness, faithfulness, gentleness and self control. If a person demonstrates these qualities, would you say that he is emotionally healthy? Certainly. And if these qualities were missing, or were seldom demonstrated, you would probably question that person's emotional health. Paul indicates that a person who lacks these qualities is not "filled with the Spirit."

John takes a very similar approach: "As we obey this commandment, to love one another, the darkness in our lives disappears and the new light of life in Christ shines in." Like Paul, John indicates that life is a struggle. You become triumphant in this struggle when "Christ lives in you." In fact, John says: "Anyone who says he is walking in the light of Christ but dislikes his fellow man, is still in darkness" (1 John 1:9). For John, emotional and spiritual health are, I believe, virtually synonymous, and you can tell when "health" has happened—you gain a deep sense of concern and love for other people.

Here is one caveat. It takes a while for this inner change to occur. A person can be filled with the Holy Spirit, and thus be spiritually healthy, while emotional health still needs to grow. The old, habituated defense patterns may take some time to dissolve.

But mark my word: When a woman and her man turn their attention to spiritual wholeness, they will be moving inevitably toward emotional health as well. You can't have one without the other.

This brings up, of course, the question of whether one can gain emotional health without being "in a right relationship with God." There are many opinions on this issue, but after all my years of clinical work, I believe that no person can get into a right relationship with themselves until they have gotten into a right relationship with God.

I've said earlier that no marriage can be truly triumphant until both parties are individually "right" with themselves. If this latter state requires a "right relationship with God," it seems obvious that a great marriage requires two people who have reached a deep level of spiritual health.

Spirituality in a Nutshell

This whole discussion about spirituality boils down to this: The world we live in every day, what we call the material world, largely involves the external—that which is outside our skin. If we try to build a great marriage that focuses exclusively on the material world, we are likely to be deeply disappointed at some point along the way. The foundation is shallow, and the painful experiences of life will have a way of washing our marriage out to sea.

Spirituality involves what is inside. It is built around a quest for deeper meaning, for a clearer sense about profound and eternal matters. Marriages that involve two people who share their experiences, thoughts, concerns, and involvement in these areas of life tend to hold together and become richer over time. These marriages usually are extremely close and ultimately healthy.

It is, then, this moving away from the material world and into the spiritual realm that takes a marriage from the superficial to the profound, from the immediate to the eternal, from two distinct individuals who merge into "one flesh." In the process, their relationship becomes stronger, larger, more colorful, and more satisfying.

The apostle John was not talking about marriage, but he was certainly talking about the spiritual when he said:

> Stop loving this evil world and all that it offers you, for when you love these things you show that you do not really love God; for all these worldly things, these evil desires—the craze for sex, the ambition to buy everything that appeals to you, and the pride that comes from wealth and importance—these are not from God. They are from this evil world itself. And this world is fading away, and these evil, forbidden things will go with it, but whoever keeps doing the will of God will live forever. (1 John 2:15-17)

Now there's a battle cry for a great marriage. Show me a marriage in which two people have taken these words seriously, and I'll show you one of those incredibly triumphant marriages—the very kind I want for you, and for all of us.

Conclusion:

Now Make It Happen

In the course of writing this book, I feel—and Marylyn agrees—that our marriage has become at least 10 percent better. I strongly hope that your reading of these 10 secrets has produced the same kind of success for your marriage.

Don't forget, most marriages are incredibly complex! You can't revolutionize them overnight, but you can move them from ordinary to magnificent over time. I have helped hundreds of couples transform their relationships, literally remodel them so that both parties were totally happy and satisfied. But it always takes time and hard work! Nothing as valuable as a great marriage is going to be delivered to you on a silver platter. You get to create it yourselves.

Start with the goal of making your marriage 10 percent better in the next 12 months. That's a goal I know you can reach. In fact, I've seldom seen two motivated partners who weren't able to accomplish this. Three things are required: (1) a deep-down willingness for your marriage to be really satisfying; (2) a thorough knowledge of exactly what is required to move your marriage forward; and (3) a clenched-jaw determination to make your marriage all that it can be.

A Deep-Down Willingness for Your Marriage to Be Really Satisfying

Many couples get stuck at whatever level of marital quality they happened to experience early in their relationship. They become convinced that this amount of satisfaction is all they can hope for. They think, *This is the way it is. I better just make the best of it.* They never aim higher because they assume there is no higher. So they stagnate. If anything, their relationship tends to deteriorate a little each year.

There are all kinds of reasons people allow "ceilings" to form regarding the quality of their marriage. I talked to a psychiatrist from my area recently about a case we're working on together. He commented on the patient's reluctance to ever have a better relationship than his parents had—like he didn't want to "show them up." The psychiatrist felt that this man quits working on his marriage when it starts getting too good.

How about you? Are you willing for your marriage to become great? Could you stand to be delighted with your primary love relationship? How do you feel about not being resentful toward your mate any longer? What would it be like to look for all of his or her virtues, instead of being eagle-eyed about faults and shortcomings? What if your marriage started growing by leaps and bounds? Would you be afraid that too much would be expected of you?

If you can say in your heart, "I am ready for my marriage to start moving toward greatness, and I'll do what it takes to make it happen," you are on the brink of an exciting adventure. If you can say this with conviction and determination, then I'm tremendously optimistic about the future of your marriage.

Whatever the current state of your marriage—miserable, boring, ordinary, average, or good—you can make it better and better over time. Step number one has everything to do with your willingness.

A Thorough Knowledge of Exactly What Is Required to Move Your Marriage Forward

This book contains everything you need to know to make your marriage triumphant. But I want to tell you something crucial: You can't read this book once and expect to have mastered all that is here. You have to read it over and over, preferably with the love of your life. You have to become familiar with the principles outlined here. And, most of all, you have to apply the information to your marriage.

Earlier I told you that these 10 secrets are the distillation of my 30 years of working with thousands of people, the wisdom of 200 spouses in extremely healthy marriages, the conclusions of scores of carefully designed research studies, my observation of the 71-year marriage of my parents, my own long-term marriage to Marylyn, my close-up examination of the marriages of many friends and my three daughters, and the reading of Jewish and Christian literature. I have complete confidence that these secrets are psychologically and spiritually accurate, that they include everything you need to make your marriage all that it can be.

Some of these secrets cannot be grasped quickly. You have to read them again and again, look at them from many angles at various points in your marriage, and talk about them with the primary persons in your life, especially your spouse.

I believe these 10 secrets fall into three categories:

1. **Emotional health.** If both you and your mate have a proper understanding of yourselves as individuals, and if you have well-developed self-concepts, the load you place on your marriage will be decidedly lighter. Marriage is not designed to make you emotionally healthy. Marriages begin to crack and crumble when the people in them want the marriage to serve in the place of God. They are simply incapable of functioning like God! Although a marital relationship can provide tremendous fulfillment, it cannot solve many of your personal problems and make you into the person you have the potential to become. But if you come to the marriage with a solid sense of yourself, a well-worked-through set of primary relationships, and a balanced inner life, you are ready for a great marriage. If you didn't come to marriage this way, you have some work to do. Do it now!

2. **Deep-down, old-fashioned, lifelong commitment.** It's almost impossible to make a marriage magnificent if the commitment of both partners isn't well-established and without question. When you marry, it takes time and hard work to build the relationship into what you want it to be. If one or both of you even occasionally reconsiders your commitment, wondering if you really want to be in this relationship, your marriage will undoubtedly be less than it could be. Commitment requires fierce determination to back it up! Fierce determination demands regular "firing up" of your dedication. Regular firing up is where rehearsal comes in. Commit yourself to your lover every single day. I guarantee it will pay off. It will settle your partner's fears and your own. As you both commit yourselves to each other over and over, you will become

confident that you have plenty of time to build the skills you need to make your marriage all you have dreamed it could be—and more!

3. **Skill building.** You need five basic skills as a couple if you want to build a great marriage: (1) you need to learn to dream together; (2) you need to learn how to communicate at a deep level together; (3) you need to learn to resolve conflict when it first occurs; (4) you need to learn to negotiate a mutually satisfying sexual relationship; and (5) you need to pursue spirituality and plumb its depths in partnership with your spouse. All of these skills are straightforward and learnable. If the two of you can become proficient at these five skills, there is no holding you back.

A Clenched-Jaw Determination to Make Your Marriage All That It Can Be

At the beginning of this book, I told you about my friend who took his tennis game from very average to incredibly good over a two-year period because he worked so hard at it. He takes four two-hour lessons a week, and he has achieved a level of mastery that is well beyond anything that he had dreamed possible.

Hear me on this! If you want your marriage to become great, and if you have read and reread everything I have said about what you need to master, the upper-limit of marital magnificence you can reach is dependent only on your determination to work hard. If you and your spouse are prepared to give it all you've got, your marriage can move inexorably toward greatness.

Having watched thousands of lives from a close-up vantage point over the years, I can tell you that I have never seen anything more exciting, more gratifying, or more helpful to others than a highly successful marriage. Show me a great marriage involving two healthy people, and I'll show you dozens of people who benefit incredibly from it.

I often think about my own parents' marriage, which lasted nearly 71 years. There are 65 members in our family, and every one of us was inspired by my parents' relationship. They were the ones who taught us about commitment and loyalty. They were the ones who convinced every one of us that we were loved in our bones and our marrow. They were the ones who showed us how to dream and envision a bigger and better future. They were the ones who taught us a faith and who lived it consistently and freely for us to see. And they were the ones whose marriage kept getting better and better the longer they lived.

What this world needs is a revolution in the area of marriage. Think what a difference a few hundred thousand more triumphant marriages would make in North America. I unashamedly encourage you and your mate to shoot for greatness in your marriage. I cheer for you to step out and move forward. You know what I know—that it will take hard work and fierce determination. But I'm convinced that the prize is supremely worth the cost!

You can do it, and if you do, the satisfaction you experience will be greater than any you have ever known before.

Twenty-five Additional Tips for Building a Triumphant Marriage

(More wisdom from the 100 extremely successful couples)

I couldn't finish this book without giving you the full benefit of our 100 surveyed couples' accumulated knowledge and experience. Their responses to my questionnaire were so rich with insights and sage advice that I simply had to pass them along. Here, then, are more pearls of wisdom from those who have mastered the art of creating long-lasting and supremely happy marriages.

1. Express your gratitude to each other until it becomes habitual.

"We decided while dating to thank each other for small, daily things we appreciated about the other (such as doing the dishes, taking out the trash, caring for the pets), and that has become a habit that encourages us to be considerate of each other. It keeps the positive feelings flowing and helps us not take each other for granted. It has generalized to our children, who also thank us quite often when they appreciate something we've done for them."

2. Work at being great friends.
"The key to our marriage is friendship. Sheila has become my best friend. Sleeping, eating, working, vacationing, playing—all with someone who provides emotional, physical, and spiritual support. Is there anything better than this?"

3. If you make your lover feel loved, you will significantly strengthen your marriage.
"The secret of a great marriage is to show your spouse every day—and even verbalize it, if necessary—how much you love her and how glad you are that you get to spend your whole life with her."

"My husband is the master of spontaneity and surprise! In everything he does, he seems to enjoy letting me know how much he loves me. I love him so much—partially because of how much he loves me."

4. Learn how to apologize and how to forgive.
"It isn't always easy to say you're sorry. But if you can admit mistakes and apologize for them, you won't give problems a chance to fester and swell."

"Some people nurture grudges and hold on to wrongs done to them. This is a sure way to drive a wedge between you and your spouse."

5. Look for all the positive qualities in your mate.
"It's incredibly easy to focus only on the negative aspects of your marriage or your mate. In doing so, however, you miss out on all the positive things. We make it a regular practice to count our blessings and talk about the other person's strengths and good qualities."

"I feel so fortunate and blessed by what I learn relationally from my husband. He is wise, sensitive, and cares deeply for me. He loves the Lord. He loves me. He loves what is important to me. He loves what is good and right."

6. Create a "working partnership" with each other.
"One of the best things about our marriage is that we have a 'working relationship.' We work incredibly well together—whether our task has to do with children, our careers, our church, or our future. We are a real partnership!"

7. Look for the changes in your marriage. They speak eloquently about the quality of your relationship.

"We have grown significantly through the years. I have become a cross-country skier, Jeff has become a family man, me a churchgoer, Jeff a helpful party-thrower, me a mountain woman, Jeff a flower giver. I can't wait to see what God does with us in the coming years. It is exciting to see what love, commitment, trust, forgiveness, hope, and faith can do in a marriage."

8. Maintain careful control over your expectations.

"My expectations for my marriage are not elaborate. I expect to go through the ups and downs of life with my spouse. I expect that we will go through difficult phases . . . but together. I expect that I will love him more and more deeply through it all. I just want to grow old knowing and loving my husband."

9. Recognize and celebrate your expectations that have been met.

"I now realize that my expectations for my marriage have been wonderfully met. I wanted Don's love, and he's given it freely. I wanted to finish college, and I did. I wanted children, and we adopted three of the best kids I could ever hope for. I wanted a house, and amazingly, we have one, despite being missionaries for a while. Now in my later years, I realize I wanted a good companion, and I have one. I don't think my life could be better!"

10. Try to grow from unmet expectations.

"Where our expectations have not been met, we have learned some valuable lessons. For instance, I expected our children to conform more to our beliefs and practices than has been the case. This has taught me a wonderful and desirable discipline—acceptance of differences."

11. Strive for "mutuality" in marriage.

"We have a relationship characterized by mutual respect and mutual enjoyment. Neither of us is self-centered in a narcissistic way. We both serve each other with a natural give-and-take that depends on the need of the moment. We are two strong individuals who have become 'one.' Mutuality is central to the success of our marriage."

12. Experience strong feelings together.

"We experience strong feelings in very similar ways. We laugh a lot at the same kinds of things and cry in the same movies. This seems to bind us to each other."

13. If you go through suffering together, it will create wonderful possibilities for your relationship.

"When my husband was so sick with cancer, God healed him and gave us the strength to get through the illness. In the movie 'Shadowlands,' after the woman he loves dies, C.S. Lewis says, 'The pain now is part of the joy then.' We feel so deeply blessed that our pain then is part of the joy now. We got a taste of what it would be like to face death and separation from each other. This gives us a richer appreciation of each day together. Also, we realize our powerlessness and attempt to surrender all to God. The spiritual connection is profound and real for us."

14. Prayer really changes things.

"We pray together and often talk about what God is doing in our lives. Prayer guides us in our goal-setting, parenting, conflict resolution, and financial plans. Every morning, we discuss challenges for the coming day, and we pray for each other throughout the day. We call each other often on days we know the other is going to struggle or worry."

"If we were starting our marriage all over again, I would spend a lot more time in prayer. I would trust in God and not worry so much."

15. Renew your commitment—especially when the going gets hard.

"Commitment is paramount! It requires each person to be responsible for the ultimate well-being and happiness of the other with no expectation that the marital relationship is a bargained-for exchange of rights, powers, privileges, and immunities."

"When we are going through particularly difficult periods, we renew our commitment by actually stating, 'I'm here with you' or 'I wouldn't want to do this with anyone else.' "

16. Make playtime a regular part of your marriage.

"One of the best things about our marriage is that we have so much fun when we're together, even if we're just hanging out and doing nothing. I feel like we could spend an indefinite period of time together without contact with anyone else and both be totally content."

"For so many years, all we did was work, work, work. Now we've learned to make time for plenty of recreation—taking walks, playing games, seeing movies, going on weekend getaways. I wish we would have played more in our earlier years."

17. Communication tends to go well if you do it right.

"We've had to work hard at listening, negotiating, compromising, telling the complete truth, and being transparent with each other. Over the years, we've become skillful in these areas, and that has greatly enhanced our marriage."

"We are pretty much open with each other, but we have learned to choose our words carefully to be as clear and thoughtful as possible. We've made an art form out of communicating so that the other person can know exactly what we're thinking and feeling."

18. Build a workable model for managing conflict with your spouse.

"We have found two qualities especially helpful in managing our conflict: (1) try not to discuss/argue at night (timing is important); (2) preface negative comments with positive ones: 'You do a great job at this, but could you please. . . .' "

"Because of my upbringing, we usually handle our conflict in the time-honored Italian way—with an argument. But it works for us. We get everything aired out, then we can work on resolving the problem."

19. Learn to share negative and positive feelings without delay.

"Neither of us can tolerate more than 20 minutes of subterranean conflict, so we force feelings into words consistently. We share the positive as well. We say 'thank you' and 'I love you' all the time."

20. Never purposefully embarrass your mate.

"There's nothing more degrading than being humiliated or put down in public. This is a sure way to start a fight with your spouse."

"One of the most important things I've learned about marriage is never to back your spouse into a corner in front of other people."

21. Whenever possible, carefully plan the future of your marriage.

"Having a five-year period to develop our marriage before we had kids really helped us get established."

"It would have saved us considerable stress and pressure if we had been

better about planning for the future. We often just let things happen.
Couples should plot a course for their lives and their marriages, and stick
with it."

22. Don't be afraid to let your children be your teachers.

"Children have been a joy and God's way of humbling us. Our children
teach us all the time. We have a great time together—sharing love, laughter,
and tears."

23. Even though you're "one flesh," your spouse is a separate person.

"I had to learn the hard way that my husband is a unique individual, a
separate person. His thoughts are his own and do not necessarily represent
my opinions or the children's. When I keep this straight, I give him signifi-
cantly more freedom to be himself. Both of us are happier this way."

24. Develop your love relationship—independently of well-meaning others.

"My husband and I believe that one of the best things that ever
happened to us was that we moved away from both of our families for the
first six years of our married life. That gave us a chance to develop our rela-
tionship—not a relationship designed to please every important person in
our lives."

25. Work to keep your love fresh.

"Keeping our love fresh and alive was a goal we set even prior to
marriage. We work hard at it. In fact, we rank it right up there at the top of
our list of goals. After all these years, I can tell you that I can hardly wait to
see my wife every night. She hugs me like she thinks I'm wonderful, too!"

Notes

LOVE SECRETS FOR A TRIUMPHANT MARRIAGE

1. Robert J. Sternberg, "A Triangular Theory of Love," *Psychological Review* 93, no. 2 (1986): 119–35 (quote is from p. 119).
2. Bureau of the Census, CPR, Series P-23, No. 162, June 1989, 3–4, and Series P-20, No. 45, June 1990, 2, 9.

SECRET #2

1. Jeanette Lauer and Robert Lauer, "Marriages Made to Last," *Psychology Today* (June 1985): 22–26.
2. Robert J. Sternberg, "A Triangular Theory of Love," *Psychological Review* 93, no. 2 (1986): 119–35 (quote is from p. 123).
3. See my book *Make Anger Your Ally*, 3d ed. (Colorado Springs, Colo.: Focus on the Family, 1990).

SECRET #5

1. Neil Clark Warren, *Finding the Love of Your Life: Ten Principles for Choosing the Right Marriage Partner* (Colorado Springs, Colo.: Focus on the Family, 1992).

SECRET #6

1. Brandt, 1982, from David Knox and Caroline Schacht, *Choices in Relationships: An Introduction to Marriage and the Family* (Saint Paul, Minn.: West Publishing Company, 1991), 298.
2. P. Noller and M. A. Fitzpatrick, "Marital Communication in the Eighties," in *Contemporary Families: Looking Forward, Looking Back,* ed. A. Booth (Minneapolis: National Council on Family Relations, 1991), 42–53.
3. S. S. Brehm, *Intimate Relationships* (New York: Random House, 1985).
4. "The 1990 Virginia Slims Opinion Poll," study conducted by the Roper Organization, Inc., Roper Center, University of Connecticut, Storrs, CN 06268.

SECRET #7

1. Murray A. Straus, Richard J. Gelles, and Suzanne Steinmetz, *Behind Closed Doors: Violence in the American Family* (Garden City, N.Y.: Doubleday, 1978).
2. J. M. Gottman and L. J. Krokoff, "Marital Interaction and Satisfaction: A Longitudinal View," *Journal of Consulting and Clinical Psychology* 57, no. 1 (1989): 47–52.
3. E. Menaghan, "Marital Stress and Family Transitions: A Panel Analysis," *Journal of Marriage and the Family* 45 (1983): 371–86.
4. John Gottman, "New Ways to Tell If Your Love Will Last," *Glamour,* Feb. 1994, 203.

SECRET #8

1. Robert T. Michael, John H. Gagnon, Edward O. Laumann, and Gina Kolata, *Sex in America: A Definitive Survey* (Boston: Little, Brown and Company, 1994).
2. Clifford L. Penner and Joyce J. Penner, *The Gift of Sex* (Waco, Tex.: Word Publishing, 1981).
3. Clifford L. Penner and Joyce J. Penner, *Restoring the Pleasure* (Waco, Tex.: Word Publishing, 1994).

SECRET #9

1. Judith Wallerstein and Sandra Blakeslee, *Second Chances: Men, Women, and Children a Decade After Divorce* (New York: Ticknor and Fields, 1990). See also "For Better, For Worse—The Growing Movement to Strengthen Marriage and Prevent Divorce," *Time,* Feb. 27, 1995.

About the Author

Neil Clark Warren is one of America's best known relational psychologists with 30 years in his own practice. He received his bachelor's degree from Pepperdine University, his Master of Divinity degree from Princeton Theological Seminary, and his Ph.D. in clinical psychology from The University of Chicago. In addition, Dr. Warren is a much sought after speaker who captivates listeners with his ability to passionately relate complex issues is a simple, practical, and easily understood format.

Dr. Warren's first book, *Make Anger Your Ally*, was heralded a "must read" by *Time* magazine. His *Finding the Love of Your Life* was an international bestseller and the 1993 recipient of a Gold Medallion award for Best Marriage book. Dr. Warren is also the author of *Learning to Live With the Love of Your Life . . . and Loving It*, which was selected in 1995 by *USA Today* as having made an outstanding contribution to the field of marriage.

A frequent guest on national television and radio programs across the country, Dr. Warren and his wife, Marylyn, live in Southern California. They have three grown daughters.

For more information regarding Dr. Warren and his books and seminars, call (626) 795-4814.

PUBLISHING

Also From Neil Clark Warren, Ph.D.
and Focus on the Family®

Finding the Love of Your Life
Whether you're starting a relationship, seriously considering marriage, or longing to find that special someone, this best-selling hardcover is for you! Full of practical insights and sage advice, it outlines the 10 proven principles that will guide you through the challenge of choosing a mate you can love *and* live with happily for a lifetime. Also available on audiocassette.

Finding the Love of Your Life Study Guide
Perfect for singles' Sunday school classes or Bible studies, this discussion-provoking companion guide will help those looking for Miss or Mr. Right make the right choice.

Make Anger Your Ally
Anger is powerful. You can suppress it, deny it, and let it control you. Or, you can learn how to manage it. Delve into this eye-opening paperback, and discover how to harness its energy to cope with pain and resolve problems. Anger—make it work for you, not against you.

• • •

Look for these books in your favorite Christian bookstore. You can also request a copy by calling 1-800-A-FAMILY or by writing Focus on the Family, Colorado Springs, CO 80995. Friends in Canada may call 1-800-661-9800 or write Focus on the Family, P.O. Box 9800, Stn. Terminal, Vancouver, B.C. V6B 4G3. Visit our Web site—www.family.org—to learn more about the ministry or to find out if there is a Focus on the Family office in your country.

8BPXMP

FOCUS ON THE FAMILY®

Welcome to the *Family!*

Whether you received this book as a gift, borrowed it from
a friend, or purchased it yourself, we're glad you read it! It's
just one of the many helpful, insightful and encouraging
resources produced by Focus on the Family.

In fact, that's what Focus on the Family is all about—
providing inspiration, information and biblically based
advice to people in all stages of life.

It began in 1977 with the vision of one man, Dr. James Dobson,
a licensed psychologist and author of 16 best-selling books
on marriage, parenting, and family. Alarmed by the societal,
political, and economic pressures that were threatening the
existence of the American family, Dr. Dobson founded
Focus on the Family with one employee—an assistant—and
a once-a-week radio broadcast, aired on only 36 stations.

Now an international organization, Focus on the Family is dedicated to
preserving Judeo-Christian values and strengthening the family
through more than 70 different ministries, including eight separate
daily radio broadcasts; television public service announcements;
11 publications; and a steady series of books and award-winning
films and videos for people of all ages and interests.

Recognizing the needs of, as well as the sacrifices and important
contribution made by, such diverse groups as educators, physicians,
attorneys, crisis pregnancy center staff and single parents, Focus on
the Family offers specific outreaches to uphold and minister to these
individuals, too. And it's all done for one purpose, and one purpose
only: to encourage and strengthen individuals and families
through the life-changing message of Jesus Christ.

• • •

For more information about the ministry, or if we can be of help to your family,
simply write to Focus on the Family, Colorado Springs, CO 80995 or call
1-800-A-FAMILY (1-800-232-6459). Friends in Canada may write Focus on the
Family, P.O. Box 9800, Stn. Terminal, Vancouver, B.C. V6B 4G3 or call
1-800-661-9800. Visit our Web site—www.family.org—to learn more about the
ministry or to find out if there is a Focus on the Family office in your country.

We'd love to hear from you!